SHAFTESBURY'S

SECOND CHARACTERS

T0371347

The Right Honourable Anthony Ashley Cooper,
Earl of Shaftesbury

Frontispiece

SECOND CHARACTERS

OR

THE LANGUAGE OF FORMS

BY THE RIGHT HONOURABLE

ANTHONY, EARL OF SHAFTESBURY
AUTHOR OF *CHARACTERISTICS*

EDITED BY

BENJAMIN RAND, PH.D.
HARVARD UNIVERSITY

Cambridge :

at the University Press

1914

CAMBRIDGE
UNIVERSITY PRESS

University Printing House, Cambridge CB2 8BS, United Kingdom

Published in the United States of America by Cambridge University Press, New York

Cambridge University Press is part of the University of Cambridge.

It furthers the University's mission by disseminating knowledge in the pursuit of education, learning and research at the highest international levels of excellence.

www.cambridge.org
Information on this title: www.cambridge.org/9781107685413

© Cambridge University Press 1914

First published 1914
First paperback edition 2014

A catalogue record for this publication is available from the British Library

ISBN 978-1-107-68541-3 Paperback

Cambridge University Press has no responsibility for the persistence or accuracy of URLs for external or third-party internet websites referred to in this publication, and does not guarantee that any content on such websites is, or will remain, accurate or appropriate.

TO

THE RIGHT HONOURABLE

ANTHONY, EARL OF SHAFTESBURY

CONTENTS

INTRODUCTION

THE Third Earl of Shaftesbury is best known to the world as the author of the 'Characteristics.' Another work by him was discovered by the present editor in the Record Office in London, and printed in 1900, with the title of 'Philosophical Regimen.' At that time a manuscript volume was also found among the Shaftesbury Papers, containing the plan and fourth treatise of a work intended as a complement to the 'Characteristics,' which was entitled 'Second Characters.' This volume was mostly written in 1712. It appears that owing to declining health Shaftesbury had been compelled to leave England and spend the last year and a half of his life in Italy. On the 3rd of July, 1711, he sailed from Dover, and proceeding slowly through Paris, Turin, and Rome, arrived November 15th, 1711, in Naples. In this city he resided, seeking in vain through the aid of a mild climate to recover his gradually failing strength, until his death, February 15th, 1713. In spite of his contest with disease, and brief as was the period that remained to him of allotted life, his last months spent in Naples were nevertheless replete with large literary activity. Not only did he then complete for the press a second edition of the 'Characteristics' but he likewise carried forward the preparation for intended publication of an entirely new work.

The book was to consist of four treatises. These were: I 'A Letter concerning Design'; II 'A Notion of the Historical Draught or Tablature of The Judgment of Hercules'; III 'An Appendix concerning the Emblem of Cebes'; and IV 'Plastics

or the Original Progress and Power of Designatory
Art.' The 'Letter concerning Design' was printed
for the first time in 1732, in the fifth edition of the
'Characteristics.' The 'Judgment of Hercules' was
first printed in French, in the *Journal des Sçavans* for
November, 1712, a fact which has heretofore strangely
escaped the attention of bibliographers. An "original
translation" of this treatise appeared in English,
separately, in 1713, and was also included in the
second edition of the 'Characteristics' in 1714. The
'Appendix concerning the Emblem of Cebes,' so far
as known, remained to be written, and the 'Tablet'
itself instead is here printed in a new translation.
'Plastics,' regarded by the author as the chief
treatise of the four, has never previously been published. The definite grouping of these various
treatises in the form of a single work, as intended
when written, is also here first made known. Just two
centuries have elapsed since Shaftesbury was forced
to lay down his pen, until the present editing, for the
first time, of his aesthetic work with the title of 'Second
Characters,' so far as it is completed.

Concerning the origin and progress of 'Second
Characters' considerable information may be gathered
from the correspondence of Shaftesbury while in
Naples. To Thomas Micklethwayt, his young friend
who carried the second edition of the 'Characteristics'
through the press after his death, he says in a post-
script to a letter of February 2nd, 1712[1]: "I must add
a word to tell you that if I live and am able to proceed
in my virtuoso studies it will follow of necessity (as
you may easily conceive) that I shall embrace more
objects in my view than simply what I first began
upon, and was the cause of my search. Is it possible
think you for me to enlarge my conversation, engage
in speculative reading and antiquities of this kind and
not find in any way many curiosities of which without

---

[1] An unpublished letter among the Shaftesbury Papers.

any more trouble and with the same expense of pains and money I may make some improvement?" Here was the inception of a new project in art, born of his surroundings, and made in addition to the preparation of the second edition of the 'Characteristics' with its newly planned emblems. "My own designs," he writes, February 16th, 1712, to his intimate friend, Sir John Cropley, "you know run all on moral emblems and what relates to ancient Roman and Greek history, philosophy and virtue. Of this the modern painters have but little taste. If anything be stirred, or any studies turned this way, it must be I that must set the wheel a going and help to raise the spirit....My charges turn wholly, as you see, towards the raising of art and the improvement of virtue in the living, and in posterity to come[1]." Like Plato, Shaftesbury realized that you must surround the citizens with an atmosphere of grace and beauty if you desire to instil noble and true ideas in the mind. And animated by the inspired purpose of reviving and elevating art, particularly in England, his remaining strength was steadfastly applied to the production of 'Second Characters.'

To Micklethwayt in a letter of February 23rd, 1712, Shaftesbury writes: "I have a noble virtuoso scheme before me, and design, if I get life this summer, to apply even this great work (the history piece bespoke, and now actually working) to the credit and reputation of Philol....I know that by what I have said I must have highly raised your curiosity, which till next post I am unable to satisfy, and then you shall have it all before you by the copy of the little treatise (which Mr Crell is now actually transcribing from the foul) written, or rather dictated, on this subject of the great piece of history in hand, and which will come within the compass of a sheet of paper. But it being

---

[1] *The Life, Unpublished Letters, and Philosophical Regimen of the Third Earl of Shaftesbury*, edited by Benjamin Rand, London, 1900, p. 468-9.

written in French for the painters use, you cannot have
it in its right condition until it be thought over anew
and translated anew into its natural English. It will
be in Mr Coste's power to make this piece truly
original, as it now is, by touching it up (as the painters'
phrase is) and converting it wholly into pure language
with his masterly hand and genius. And in this
condition I would willingly consent he should carry it,
or send it over to his friend to be inserted in the very
next *Bib. Chois.* of his friend's friend Mons. Le Clerc[1]."
The historical piece, to which reference is here made,
was the Choice of Hercules, as related by Prodicus
and recorded by Xenophon in the second book of the
Memorabilia, of which Shaftesbury had undertaken to
have a painting made by Paulo de Matthaeis. In
order that the painter might have full information in
regard to the purpose of the fable and the desired
character of the work, the "little treatise" above mentioned was written and was composed in French as he
says "from what passed in conversation with my
painters, and some other virtuosos with whom I can
converse only in that language." On the first appearance of the 'Judgment of Hercules' in French, in the
Journal des Sçavans, Nov., 1712, he judged an early
translation and publication of it in English to be
necessary, as he was doubtless mindful of his previous
experience in the surreptitious issue of the 'Inquiry
concerning Virtue.' "With extreme satisfaction," he
writes to Pierre Coste, November 22nd, 1712, "I have
just now received the three exemplars of the little
dissertation in which your admirable judgment and
care has made me not a little proud, so that I am in a
manner resolved to naturalize it myself and give it to
the public Englished at first hand, rather than suffer it
to go to Grub Street by help of those Anglo-Gallish
translators, who generally understand neither the one
language nor the other[2]." The English publication of

---

[1] *Ibid.* p. 472–3.   [2] *Ibid.* p. 523.

this treatise was also deemed urgent by his friends. "I join with you," he writes to Micklethwayt, December 20th, 1712, "in opinion for instantly printing the 'Judgment of Hercules' as I wrote to you and Sir John just before I fell ill, and having presently made my plan you will receive it from Mr Crell transcribed by the next post that Mr D—y may instantly proceed[1]." And in a final letter of January 10th, 1713, to Micklethwayt he concludes : " I hope I may soon by the posts receive from you the return of the models of the title-pages, and perhaps the first sheet of the 'Judgment of Hercules' if you have resolution enough to print at least the 'Notion' by itself, to which singly (as I wrote you) the advertisement I first sent (in mine of December 27) may serve as a preface leaving out only the last words, viz. 'in the letter which is here prefixed'." These letters reveal very clearly the reason and circumstances which led to the separate publication of the 'Judgment of Hercules' in 1712, in anticipation of the completed work of 'Second Characters.' There is, moreover, no evidence of any intention on the part of Shaftesbury ever to print this treatise as part of the 'Characteristics,' and it, with the 'Letter of Design,' has been very properly omitted by Mr J. M. Robertson in his excellent edition of that classic work.

To Lord Somers all the treatises which comprise the 'Characteristics' had been dedicated by Shaftesbury. It was only natural therefore in the gradual development of his new literary project that 'The Notion' should be accompanied by a letter to his esteemed patron. The first reference to this dedicatory epistle is to be found in a letter of March 29th, 1712, to Sir John Cropley. "You have here," he says, " enclosed my letter [of Design] long promised, and (as you see) long since written to our old Lord [Somers]. The little treatise [or 'Judgment of Hercules'] which

[1] *Ibid.* p. 528.

accompanies it (and which I hope you will deliver or convey carefully and handsomely sealed up with it) I have also enclosed this post to my cousin Mick[1]." On the 12th of April, he writes to Micklethwayt: "And earnestly I long (as you may well believe) to hear of the delivery, reception, and success of my epistle [of Design] and treatise [of Hercules] thereto belonging." Shaftesbury's first intention when he thought of making an English translation of the 'Judgment of Hercules' was to include in its publication the 'Letter of Design.' "Now pray tell me," he writes, November 22nd, 1712, to Sir John Cropley, "which I had better resolve to do? Whether leave it ['Judgment of Hercules'] to the Grub Street translators and retailers to rend in their own game, or whether produce the *original translation* (if I may call it) by itself alone without that which I count the life and spirit of it I mean the recommendatory letter [of Design] to my friend-lord, whose property this is, and to whom it is my chief delight to join myself, in these as in former thoughts and contemplations of my retired and leisured hours. For my own part should the Lord approve the thing I am resolute to send both 'Letter' and 'Notion' without more ado to Darby (suppressing names only), to be printed in the very manner and character as the 'Letter of Enthusiasm'[2]." Among his last instructions concerning the publication contained in an unpublished manuscript he quotes from a letter to Mr M—t of the 3rd of January, 1713: "If you friends, who are judges of the affair, cannot resolve to print the 'Letter' itself together with the 'Notion, I hope at least you may hold the resolution of printing the 'Notion' to save the abuse of a Grub Street translation." His friends Micklethwayt and Cropley brought out the 'Judgment of Hercules' in 1712, as we have seen, but they did not print the 'Letter of Design.' Doubtless the inclusion of the 'Notion' in

---

[1] *Ibid.* p. 781-2.   [2] *Ibid.* p. 526-7.

the second, third, and fourth editions of the 'Characteristics' aroused the desire to have all the treatises of
the author then known to exist, in this work, and led
to the printing in its fifth edition of the 'Letter of
Design' in the incongruous position of a closing
treatise. But in the phrase in the present volume,
"Observe also if the 'Letter' and 'Notion' be first
printed and afterward the whole together under the
answerable general title of 'Second Characters'"
Shaftesbury looks forward to the publication of this
completed work. For the first time therefore the
'Letter of Design' now appears, as intended, at the
beginning as a real epistle of dedication to his friend,
Lord Somers.

Already in February of 1712 the thoughts of
Shaftesbury had turned towards 'The Tablet of Cebes'
as capable of somewhat similar artistic and literary
treatment to that he had in hand upon the 'Judgment
of Hercules.' He expresses the desire at that time
that Mr Coste be instructed "to bring with him from
Holland the best edition or two (with notes) of Cebes'
Table, with the ordinary ugly prints (such as there are)
of this beautiful socratic piece, which I shall have
time to study at leisure and fit for a companion to this
other socratic, but more simple, and (in painting) more
exact, natural, and just piece of Prodicus now carrying
on, and upon which I have composed my little treatise
in French[1]." An engraving had been made of the
painting of Hercules illustrating the tale of Prodicus
and there was a first vague notion that one of Cebes
might accompany it for insertion in the 'Characteristics'
(vol. II, p. 250) in connection with the reference to Cebes
and Prodicus. Later, however, the idea of its proper
place as part of a new treatise developed. "And now
Cebes," he writes in April to Sir John Cropley, "may
follow in due time, if my life goes beyond this summer,
and that I live to see the beginning of another." And

[1] *Ibid.* p. 474.

b 2

again to Pierre Coste, who had not yet visited Naples, he says in a letter of July 25th : " Pray if you light on any good edition, private or particular remarks, notes or thoughts on Cebes' Table, pick them up and bring them improved to me by your reflections[1]." Shaftesbury did not live to see another summer and probably never wrote the 'Appendix concerning the Emblem of Cebes.' Among his manuscripts in the Record Office, however, there is an English translation of Cebes' 'Tablet' with notes, that has never been published. The translator writes in easy flowing English, unimpeded by the Greek forms of the original text. The accuracy with which every thought of the Greek author is reproduced indicates too that the translator like Shaftesbury was a master of the classics. But the translation is not in Shaftesbury's handwriting and if it were by him must have been dictated. The Notes to the translation might possibly also be by him, as the language and thought bear such a close resemblance to the contents of a letter written to Pierre Coste[2]. It is this translation of the 'Tablet of Cebes' with notes which appears in the present work in lieu of the unwritten 'Appendix' to it.

The fourth treatise, that on 'Plastics,' is styled by Shaftesbury the "great one" of 'Second Characters.' It is to be found in a manuscript volume of 'The Shaftesbury Papers' (V. 15) in the London Record Office. At the beginning of this volume there is also outlined the plan and directions for the union of the four treatises here mentioned as composing 'Second Characters.' The date of the proposed scheme of the entire work is April 25th, 1712, which would probably precede a direct accumulation of data for the chief treatise. Writing to Pierre Coste at Amsterdam, July 25th, 1712, concerning the French copy of the 'Judgment of Hercules' he gives a reason for its publication that bears directly upon the larger

---

[1] *Ibid.* p. 525.   [2] *Ibid.* p. 359.

project. "If the piece," he says, "were found valuable I could freely commit it to you, and the author being *for the present* unknown (no matter what happened afterwards) I should be content to see it abroad in any journal. That of Monsieur Le Clerc's would be too high honour for it perhaps. The reason why I wish this is because I should, from the effect of this when it was read by people of fashion, be able to judge whether or no it would be worth while to turn my thoughts (as I am tempted) towards the further study of design and plastic art, both after the ancient and modern foundations, being able (as I myself) to instil by this means some further thoughts of virtue and honesty, and the love of liberty and mankind, after a way wholly new and unthought of[1]." His friends were always anxious lest these constant labours should destroy any chance he had of recovery, and for this reason he constantly sought to minimize the extent and importance of his work. "As I once told my cousin Mick," he writes, October 11th, 1712, to Sir John Cropley, "very emphatically, 'tis easier to write Characters than Char-acks. My trifles of virtuosoship are all I should entertain you with, and if this prove not entertaining or profiting (I should hope) some little moral along with them. The mighty treatises [Cebes and Plastics] which you seem to think me intent upon (according to report from cousin Mick) are barely two such poor tracts as the 'Letter' and 'Notion,' already sent through your heads to our old Lord. Nor have I yet set pen to paper, or dictated one word on either of these intended pieces, only noted a few memorandums, that if I should live over the winter I might employ myself a little during the following summer[2]." Doubtless the author would not have included in the publication of the book the early "memorandums" which are printed in this text under the 'Title' and 'Idea of the Work' and 'Prefatory Anticipatory Thoughts to each piece

[1] *Ibid.* p. 503.   [2] *Ibid.* p. 518.

severally.' They throw, however, so much light upon
the relation of the 'Characteristics' to the 'Second
Characters,' and give the reader such intimacy with
the author in his study, that it is believed their insertion
will much enhance the interest and value of the present
work.

With unflagging zeal Shaftesbury henceforward
applied himself to the completion of his literary task.
To Sir John Cropley he writes in an unpublished
letter, dated November 8th, 1712: "I have promised
to treat him [i.e. Micklethwayt] less like a disciple, and
hope that as a friend he will not find the same uneasiness in corresponding with me, especially on the
subjects of virtuosoship and the new ornaments of my
first offspring (as I have called it) which I had never set
about with such application of labour, and time so scarce
with me at this time of day, but for his importunity
and earnest exhortation ever since I left England.
These indeed are now become my only remaining
study. Tho perhaps out of these amusements I may
raise something which may help still to recommend my
former offspring; this being all I meant by the four
treatises with which you were so alarmed by my cousin
Mick, as taking them to be really four new philosophical pieces in the same strain with Philol. But
for such study as that would imply I have (God
knows), but very insufficient health and strength.
Some memoirs and transactions of affairs, which I once
acted in, and characters I well know, might possibly
employ my pen at thoughtful hours in the public.
And these might be of weight when I am dead, tho at
present you tell me men laugh at characters and
secrets, and despise what we poor writers may compose.
Be it so." One has only to read the passages in his
letters with reference to his now rapidly failing health
to discover what bravery was involved in these final
efforts. "The more painful my hours grow," he writes
near the close to Micklethwayt, January 3rd, 1713,
"and the fewer I have to expect in life, the faster you

see I ply you (and shall continue to do so) with what
alone can give me amusement, and at the same time
advance the principal good I shall leave behind me,
my brain offspring, so likely to make its way, espoused
and honoured as it now is by such judgments and
friends appearing in its behalf[1]." Soon after, he was
compelled to lay down his pen. His noble spirit
passed away February 15th, 1713. Two centuries
from the period of its composition his treatise on
'Plastics' is here given to the world precisely as it
was left[2]. The queries in the text and the footnotes
will indicate the various changes or additions that
would have been made in the final writing of it for the
press. These will be found to relate chiefly to appropriate illustrations or the enlargement of certain topics.
For the most part they concern the form rather than
the content. It is therefore safe to say that the
essential thoughts of 'Plastics' are contained in the
present publication, for the first time, of this fourth
treatise of 'Second Characters.'

From the foregoing sketch of the production of
the several treatises which compose 'Second Characters' we turn to outline briefly their content. As
already remarked the 'Letter of Design' addressed to
Lord Somers now assumes its proper place at the
beginning of the volume instead of following as heretofore the 'Judgment of Hercules.' Of these two
treatises Thomas Fowler in his 'Shaftesbury and
Hutcheson' regards the 'Letter' as perhaps the more
interesting. It contains an account from Shaftesbury's
own hand of the growth and purpose of his virtuoso
work in Italy. Its inception was due, it is said, to a
conversation with his noble patron, and its final aim is
described as the revival of art, particularly in England.
The most striking feature of it is an abiding faith in
liberty and in the artistic judgment of the people as the

[1] *Ibid.* p. 529.
[2] The necessary modernisation of the text and bracketed editorial
matter must be excepted.

true foundation of any revival in liberal arts. Persistent efforts, he argues, must therefore be made, with the growing freedom, to secure the best models, to seek correct standards, and to found academies of instruction, in order to create a cultivated taste in the general public.

In the 'Notion of the Historical Draught or Tablature of the Judgment of Hercules,' Shaftesbury delineates for the benefit of his painter the scene in which Hercules according to Prodicus made a choice between the two goddesses virtue and vice. He formulates in it the rules both of consistency and of the unity of time for the correct representation of such an event in a painting. The position, pose, and habit of the principal figures, which would best maintain the truth alike of appearance and of history in the scene, are fully described. Harmony in the ornamentation is emphasized. In conclusion, a comparison is made between the task of the painter and of the poet. It was this treatise, doubtless in its French original of 1712 as well as in the German translation[1] of 1759, that had such an important influence upon aesthetics on the continent of Europe. According to Professor Howard not only does Shaftesbury present here the fullest treatment of the 'fruitful moment,' before Lessing, but he was the first among all the writers of art to consider "the pictorial value of the various moments in the course of which an action takes place[2]." He anticipated in it also, it is said, both Diderot and Lessing, in important rules given by them for the guidance of the painter, as likewise in the description of the same subject by literary and pictorial art.

In the allegory of the 'Tablet of Cebes,' with deceit at the gateway leading men astray by a draught of ignorance and error, with fortune, blind, distracted,

[1] In the *Bibliothek der Schönen Wissenschaften und der freien Künste.*

[2] *Laokoon : Lessing, Herder, Goethe.* Selections edited with an Introduction by William Guild Howard, N. Y., 1910, p. lxxvii.

and deaf, upon a round stone, her gifts being neither
certain nor stable, with true learning, upon a firm
square stone as affording alone a solid foundation
against error, and with the way to true knowledge
rough, rocky, and difficult, in contrast to the opposite
path of false knowledge, alike easy and smooth, there
are presented materials which would have afforded
Shaftesbury opportunities for literary and artistic
creation that might have rivalled those he found in the
apologue of 'Hercules at the Cross-roads.' "For
here," writes Diogenes Laertius, upon whose testimony
the authorship by Cebes chiefly depends, "thou hast a
fair prospect and view of the life of man even from the
cradle to the grave. In these few sheets thou mayest
plainly perceive with what joys and trophies a religious
man is crowned; and on the contrary with what scorn
and derision, infamy and punishment, a foolish and
wicked man is most deservedly treated." The principal
doctrines set forth in the 'Tablet' are strictly socratic.
They embrace the identity of virtue and knowledge,
the insufficiency of sense knowledge or opinion, and
the advocacy of rigorous definition. If Shaftesbury
had lived to write 'An Appendix concerning the
Emblem of Cebes,' it undoubtedly would have had an
exposition of these socratic doctrines as he expressly
mentions "after the like moral parts have been explained," and most probably would also have included
similar additional rules and observations upon art to
those set forth in the 'Notion.' "Dwell upon the
things that have been told you until they are habitual"
is an instruction in art which in more than one instance
is quoted from the 'Cebes' Tablet' in the concluding
treatise of this book. 'Ανέχειν καὶ ἀπέχειν (to bear and
to forbear), based upon the familiar words of Epictetus,
was the maxim chosen by him for the proposed treatise
and is here used with the discovered translation of the
'Emblem.' So constantly is the 'Tablet of Cebes'
before his mind, and so interwoven is it with the composition of the entire work, that this unpublished

translation of it accompanied by notes among the
'Shaftesbury Papers' is here inserted, we hope justly,
in lieu of the unwritten 'Appendix' as the third treatise
of 'Second Characters.'

'Plastics or the Original Progress and Power of
Designatory Art' is the full title of the fourth and
concluding treatise of this book. "Remember still,"
writes Shaftesbury, "this the idea of the work, viz.
quasi, the vehicle of other problems, i.e. the precepts,
demonstrations etc. of real ethics. But this hid, not to
be said except darkly or pleasantly with raillery upon
self, or some such indirect way as in 'Miscellany'."
That Shaftesbury's theory of ethics may be readily
transformed into a theory of aesthetics has been
clearly pointed out by Prof. Fowler in his work on
'Shaftesbury and Hutcheson.' In the 'Characteristics'
there is presented the Greek conception that harmony
and proportion are the ultimate foundations alike of
beauty and of morality. Man is gifted with the innate
power to recognise the beautiful alike in works of art
and in moral actions. Such a sense applied to external
objects is the sense of beauty, and applied to conduct
or disposition is the moral sense. Beauty is never in
the matter, but solely in the art or design. Art is that
which beautifies "so that the beautifying not the
beautified is the really beautiful." In the early sections
of 'Plastics' a transition is made from aesthetic
theory to applied art. The counterpart of 'First
Characters' is to be found in 'Second Characters.'
The former is speculative, the latter practical. The
'Second Characters' correspond as it were to the
underparts of a drama. And through these underparts
it is hoped to support those higher. Nevertheless, it
is added, no one may presume to criticise the 'Second
Characters' who is not already master in the First.
'Second Characters' as here described are also moral.
In proof thereof numerous quotations from classic
literature are made. Horace's *De Arte Poetica* is
most frequently cited. Painting too must be regarded

as an imitative art. It presents a picture and not
reality. Truth in it is not so much a copy of reality as
of appearance. Its poetic qualities are best found in
an historic painting such as the ' Judgment of Hercules,'
where the passions and character of men are represented. In every designatory work of art there is
something which answers to history in a truly poetic
work. This is its character : " The characteristic still,
the truth, the historic is all in all. The thing imitated,
the thing specified, is the whole delight, the secret
charm of the spectacle." All art thus deals with the
typical, or in other words the ideal.

There is next in ' Plastics' a defence of the part
played by instinct and natural sagacity as the source
of the idea of the beautiful. The corruptions of taste
are pointed out. In art as in real life a correct taste
must be cultivated. The absence of a classic environ-
ment and the substitution of the artificial for the
natural are among the discouragements of modern art.
Art ideals must to-day be sought chiefly in nature,
and in good models found in ancient remains. Among
present encouragements to art, however, is the possible
training of the public eye owing to the invention of
prints, etching, etc. A peculiar interest attaches to
the author's criticisms upon ancient and modern
painters owing to the time and place in which this
work was written. The toil, study, and meditation
necessary in the production of a great work of art are
emphasized in his remarks upon the education of the
painter. The various kinds and subjects of painting
are also discussed at considerable length. Under
the heading of the ' Revival of Second Characters'
Shaftesbury again strikes the keynote of the entire
treatise. He says that "politeness always holds proportion with laws and liberty, so that where the one is
with a tolerable progress in the first species (viz. 1st
Characters), the other (viz. 2nd Characters) will soon
prevail, and where it ceases and tyranny prevails, art
and 2nd Characters accordingly sink." Invention,

symmetry, colouring, expression, and composition,
which are the five parts of painting as observed by the
ancients and followed in the more modern works of
Junius and Fréart, are in turn discussed. The nature
and value of perspective in art form the underlying
theme of several important sections. Plastic truth and
decorum are deemed as with Plato the culminating
excellence of artistic production. The entire treatise
of 'Plastics' confirms the statement which has been
based upon the 'Judgment of Hercules,' that there can
be applied to Shaftesbury what Lessing says of
Raphael, "that he would have been the greatest
artistic genius even though unfortunately he had been
born without hands."

A true virtuoso was Shaftesbury. In the 'Characteristics' he himself delights to draw a parallel
between the philosophers and the virtuosi. "To
philosophize," he says, "in a just signification is but to
carry good breeding a step higher. For the accom-
paniment of breeding is to learn whatever is decent
in company, or beautiful in arts; and the sum of
philosophy. In this latter general denomination we
include the real fine gentleman, the lovers of art and
ingenuity, such as have seen the world, and informed
themselves of the manners and customs of the several
nations of Europe, searched into their antiquities and
records, considered their police laws, and constitutions,
observed the strength and ornaments of their cities,
their principal arts, studies and ornaments, their
architecture, sculpture, painting, music, and their taste
in poetry, learning, language and conversation."
What is here described as the "sum of philosophy" in
the artistic realm found an actual fulfilment in the
closing drama of Shaftesbury's life when he was engaged
in writing the 'Second Characters.' But the highest
examples of art belonged as he believed to the classical
period. The ancients best provided the consummate
models in art, suitable for any age. That is one
secret of his adverse criticism of the "Gothic" and the

modern. The literature of the classical authors had entered too most deeply into the warp and woof of his life. His was no mere imitation, however, of Greek and Roman thought, for he was thoroughly original both in thinking and writing. Not since the days of Plato has there been such an eloquent expression as that in the 'Characteristics[1],' of the true, the beautiful, and the good. " What is beautiful is harmonious and proportionable ; what is harmonious and proportionable is true ; and what is at once both beautiful and true is of consequence agreeable and good." Philosophy and aesthetics nevertheless meant more to him than mere theoretical systems. They must be carried over into the life of the community. The knowledge and practice of art must penetrate every province of public activity. "Where then is beauty or harmony to be found ? How is this symmetry to be discovered and applied ? Is it any other art than that of philosophy, or the study of universal numbers and proportions, which can exhibit this in life[2] ? " Through ' Second Characters ' he would emphasize the necessity that the subtle influence of beauty and art must pervade the state if its citizens would possess right ideas and exhibit noble conduct. The artistic should also permeate the whole nature of the individual. Only in this way can human achievement be glorified. Beauty is in the creator and not in the created. And beautiful products of art best serve to inspire the state of mind which the original artist experienced in creating them. Shaftesbury himself indeed was a great artist, for his whole being was permeated by the artistic temperament. He embodied the classical ideals in his own person. In outward appearance the painting of Closterman is a true portrait of him. He is the greatest Greek of modern times. It is no wonder that he appealed to the best spirits of the eighteenth century. Herder speaks of him as the " virtuoso of

---

[1] Vol. III, p. 182.   [2] *Ibid.* III, p. 184.

humanity." Montesquieu says that "the four great poets are Plato, Malebranche, Shaftesbury, Montaigne." Lessing also was a student of his works to which he had been guided by the philosopher Mendelssohn. Leibnitz too recognised in his doctrines the similarity to those he promulgated[1], and was charmed by the eloquence of his utterance. In future generations wherever there is refinement and true culture the influence of this modern classical philosopher must likewise be felt. He embodied his philosophy in a life. This philosophy finds expression in the personal meditations of the 'Philosophical Regimen,' in the moral and aesthetic doctrines of the 'Characteristics,' and in the support given to this chief work by an application of its theoretical principles to the realm of art in 'Second Characters.'

The name of Shaftesbury has been honoured in the past by the genius and the services of three distinguished members of this noble family. The first Earl was a great statesman, the third Earl an eminent philosopher, and the seventh a broad-minded philanthropist. It is a pleasure therefore to dedicate this work by permission to the present Earl, who also "has proven true to his own and his family motto, LOVE, SERVE."

[1] Their relation is best set forth in Armand Bacharach's *Shaftesbury's Optimismus und sein Verhältnis zum Leibnizschen*, Thann, 1912.

BENJAMIN RAND

HARVARD UNIVERSITY
December, 1913

SECOND CHARACTERS

OR

THE LANGUAGE OF FORMS

IN

FOUR TREATISES

viz.

I. LETTER CONCERNING DESIGN

II. A NOTION OF THE HISTORICAL
DRAUGHT OF HERCULES

III. AN APPENDIX CONCERNING THE
EMBLEM OF CEBES

IV. PLASTICS,
or THE ORIGINAL PROGRESS AND
POWER OF DESIGNATORY ART

TITLE

MEMᵈ. The frontispiece, design and motto to be the same plate as Char-cks

This absolutely determined because of mutual resemblance (*viz.* Ch-cks and Second Characters). No need of by the author of Ch.

RUNNING TITLES

GENERAL TITLE

SECOND CHARACTERS
OR
THE LANGUAGE OF FORMS
IN
FOUR TREATISES
viz.

The old round device with

Πάντα ὑπόληψις

I. A LETTER CONCERNING DESIGN

LETTER CONCERNING DESIGN

ME REBUS¹
(with the Parcae as in marg.)
sequentem ducunt nolentem trahunt

II. A NOTION OF THE HISTORICAL DRAUGHT OF HERCULES

THE HERCULES OF PRODICUS

potiores²
With the single figure and trivium by Mr Frei in a long oval

III. APPENDIX CONCERNING THE EMBLEM OF CEBES

EMBLEM OF CEBES

ἀνέχειν καὶ ἀπέχειν
with the single figure of virtue (from the best metals)

IV. PLASTICS OR THE ORIGINAL PROGRESS AND POWER OF DESIGNATORY ART

PLASTIC ART
and the particular title of this last treatise to run thus:
PLASTICS
IN
AN EPISTOLARY* EXCURSION
IN
THE ORIGINAL PROGRESS
AND
POWER OF DESIGNATORY ART

ὅ τι καλὸν φίλον ἀεί
(with the three graces)

* See the reason, *infra*, p. 5.

General motto and device same as formerly in Charck.

The particular titles (with their plates†, if so thought fit) to stand just answerably to Char-cks. Titles there being single only for the Treatises.

1 2 See notes on next page.

† i.e. in a 2nd set, not the first where (according to the precedent) only one plate, viz. the round one for a premising and experiment.

R.

I

¹ For first Treatise (viz. Letter of Design) in an oval set lengthwise (because of the design so requiring it) ME REBUS and *sequentem ducunt nolentem trahunt*. This in respect of my sickness, retreat, banishment, and secondary employment and study in Second Characters, according to the tone of the Letter of Design, parag. 4.

A chariot and the three parcae, and one riding, spinning; two drawing, with circular snare and scythes in their hands; a ragged slave chained behind, etc. On the right hand of the chariot, as it runs from left to right (of the reader), a forward figure (viz. the volens subjungens) accompanying. And remember if this succeed and be approved with the rest (viz. the 9 new plates in 2nd ed. of Char-cks) then, should I live so long, I might, in a 2nd ed. of these Second Characters at the end, subjoin (according to a previous advertisement additional in the forepart) in explanation of this and of its fellow, viz. πάντα ὑπ δλημνς in Char-cks. Beginning in English, but going off into Latin: when arrived at the authorities and citations supporting the sense of this new motto ME REBUS: according (I may say) to which I find writ in the margin of my Horace, when I first came to read him over as a man and a scholar, knowing in some measure in philosophy and Horace originals, the Socratics, and succeeding Socratic philosophy††, Horace's first and last school. And hereupon introduce (in the smallest print) the Latin Pathologia (upon Horace), or scheme of the passions in latin still, because not capable to reduce the words, and besides (as the citations) intelligible only to latin scholars. This Pathologia will be also principally grounded and supported in the explanation of the emblem treatise of Cebes, and his stoical, truly socratic δόγμα. This motto of the ME REBUS may stand in the front of this treatise notwithstanding any explanation of it in the notes of the next treatise (viz. Cebes) following after, especially since the other motto of volentem ducunt, nolentem trahunt is to stand round the figure in the plate.

Finally resolved "to seek a new moral and personally applicable motto to this leading epistle; since both the ME REBUS and the volentem ducunt must serve as supports and explanatory to one another in the device of the plate itself: the one round the edge (as πάντα ὑπόλ.), the other straight in length at the bottom under the feet of the figures.
Here it is—ante omnia Musae. VIRG. *Georg.* Lib. 2.
²

potiores
Herculis aerumnas credat, saevosque labores,
Et Venere, et coenis, et pluma Sardanapali.
JUVENAL, *Satire* x. 360.

†† Cf. *Characteristics*, III. pp. 202, 248 et II. p. 224.

LOVE   SERVE   S.Gribelin sculp

PREFACE

OF the accidental origin and general growth of
the following tracts, as well as of their corresponding with the general title which is given them, the
reader will soon be resolved and best informed as he
proceeds. If our author, who treated formerly of
CHARACTERS in a higher sense, should by this latter
manner appear to have lost somewhat of the rank he
had amidst the order of writers, this will be of small
concern to him. It is sufficient honour if by these
SECOND CHARACTERS, or under-parts, he can be able
in the least degree to support those higher, which he
once sustained in behalf of the chief concerns and
interests of mankind. The subjects which he here
treats are presumed (he knows) to relate no further
than to the ordinary pleasures and diversions of the
fashionable world. But however they may have been
rated ; if our author should by good fortune have been
able to render them more speculative, or in reality
more suitable to a taste and judgment than they have
hitherto passed in the world, he may have reason
perhaps to be satisfied with his attempt. He may
count it his happiness that whilst even he afforded

himself these entertainments for his own sake he could even in retirement find means to share them still with others, and serve the polite world and better sort in those pleasures and diversions which they are sometimes at a loss how to defend against the formal censors of the age.

" That the writings to which the author refers are perfect, or (as they ought to be) correct... is what he no way pretends. But that he has endeavoured to make them such by elaborate care and study he readily professes ; far contrary to that humour so generally affected of writing negligently and in such a manner as might easily admit of alteration and improvement by the same hand. And this profession ('tis plain) gives him (a modern) the same right as ancient[1] poets and prose authors had of saying the very same things over when occasion offered in the selfsame words[2]."

IDEA OF THE WORK

[A. PREFACES.] Again before the great Treatise remember a like small preface, or preliminary lines of introduction, To my Lord *** : that excuse may be renewed, the ridicule again anticipated ; the *moralist* or grave author vindicated and reader prepossessed ; and that the address afterwards may be more general, not always particular to that Lord : the piece being too large and too formal for a letter. Accordingly begin thus (from the first words of the Letter of Design) : "You may remember my Lord, I began this research by calling painting a vulgar science. Now you see it is come so far and I have so deeply engaged that I am about to show this to be far from a vulgar or low science."

---

[1] Such as Homer and Xenophon.
[2] Now remember this, viz. Resolved that it would be better (after this early apology in the Preface) on no account (except by necessary illustration) to refer by figures or numbers to the passages of Char-ks rehearsed. Italic characters or guillemets will be sufficient distinction.

Upon mature thought, (from consideration of the necessary repetition of the ego[1] in cases of master's hands, and what seen and observed in Italy, as also of the easy pleasant narrative manner), resolved to address wholly, or at least principally, and in a continued strain at the head of each great division, to the friend-Lord, My Lord *** as Letter of Enthusiasm and that of Design (the leading treatise of this work). And thus every new part or chapter will have a kind of preface, or renewal of the address and epistolary[2] style (My Lord, etc.). And therefore the Treatise itself should be entitled *epistolary* as giving warning of this mixed manner, viz. half-general address, but (begging the public's pardon) more than one half to the friend, the Lord, etc. Accordingly it will be a new and not odd or unseemly way to begin each great division as Book or Part (but rather Part, indeed, since Books would be too formal to divide into and contrary to the epistolary idea), to begin I say each Part with the title, My Lord, set (as at the beginning of the Letter of Enthusiasm and every other Letter) a little way below the contents. And for the subdivisions, and mere chapters or sections, these may begin not directly with the title but taking it in, (as the newer and more fashionable way is, in familiar letters), indirectly and curiously, in the first sentence or period after a word or two, (as "Would one imagine[3] My Lord" etc.). And thus the division and subdivision will be agreeable, distinguished, and in the composition of the writing and style. I shall myself be thus forced to observe a right rule, viz.: "To begin each Part with a deeper breath, distinguishably from the subaltern sallies or excursions in the mere sections into which the main parts are divided."

(1) Of this explanation of Second Characters and reasons at large see below, p. 94, in Characters, etc.

---

[1] *Infra*, p. 8.   [2] *Supra*, p. 1.
[3] Or, "It may be objected my Lord," etc. See such an objection as this : fit for the beginning of a pretty early subdivision, *infra*, p. 15.

(2)   Also apology[1] for self-citation[2], and references so frequent to Notion, Letter, and to Characteristics. Light and instruction being aimed at, and the shortest way the best.   This best too for inculcating the great maxims as from certain postulates, axioms, etc.

(3)   Motto or device of last treatise ὅ τι καλὸν φίλον ἀεί. Euripides' *Bacch.* 881.

(4)   Advertisement at the beginning of all, wishing the reader (if he would read in earnest) to observe the reference marks: as Tr. (for treatise), c (for chapter), or p (for paragraphs).   The capital figures after Tr.; small ones after c and p, and for the notes of the chapters or paragraphs the Greek characters α, β, γ, δ. In this advertisement also warning of words, phrases (see Dictionary[3]), and references to the indexes and explanations at the end of the work.

(5)   Running titles, viz. : The Letter concerning Design, The Hercules of Prodicus, Emblem[4] of Cebes. And for the title of the fourth and last work (viz. the great one) Plastic Art[5].

Let it be perhaps after the idea of *noctes atticae*, evening   conversations,   hours,   virtuoso-amusement, plastic-entertainments. *Deliciae elegantiae artis.*

(6)   The print (when all the four together) to be the same, but letters set a little closer than in Char-cks, for room (much wanting) as well as beauty, if they will be exact in setting.   The text margin to have only hands and notes and references.   But the margin of the notes to have note upon note : as Mons[r] Bayle.

[B. STYLE.]   Remember still, this the idea of the work, viz. : *Quasi.* The vehicle of other problems, i.e. the precepts, demonstrations, etc. of real ethics. But this hid : not to be said except darkly or pleasantly with raillery upon self ; or some such indirect way as in Miscellany.

Of this deviation, transfer, transition, or tralation

---

[1] *Supra*, p. 4.   [2] *Infra*, p. 12.
[3] *Infra*, p. 179.   [4] Viz. Appendix. *Supra*, p. xviii.
[5] *Supra*, p. xviii.

in favour of the τὸ καλὸν of the chief species see example below p. 142 near the end: "Accordingly the proficient" etc.

Continuance of manner and style of Miscellanys, anticipation raillery[1] etc.

And since dialogue-manner (whether diverse or recitative) too ponderous and vast; endeavour though in the letter-style and particular private address, (as O Theophilus! My Lord or Reader!), to introduce scenes and machines of this sort in many a chapter and everywhere in general, as much as possible in way of apostrophe and prosopope.

[C. INDEXES.] (1) After finis an index with this previous N.B. viz. "That the words marked with an asterisk are such as have a further explanation in the volumes entitled Charact-cks, and may be sought in the index belonging to those volumes."

(2) After this and the index make a column with this title: "Places of the volumes entitled 'Characteristics' explained or defended in this volume or 'Second Characters.'"

(3) After this again in small print and in coarse, according to the pages of the book, page after page, comprise all the translations of Greek, Latin, French, Italian, with prefatory excuse in a word or two: "as serving either for such artists in a modern way as are not scholars in the ancient, or for such scholars in the learned and ancient way as are not acquainted with the foreign modern tongues, viz. Italian or French."

(4) To have several indicatory small pointing hands (besides asterisks, daggers, etc.) wrought and cast by a good workman: that both for right and left margin there may be enough to serve for the maxims of the art, which alone are to be thus marked, as must be explained to the reader in the advertisement already mentioned[2].

(5) Also a kind of prefatory dictionary[3] of terms of art, or new coined (with apology), after the manner

---

[1] *Infra*, p. 140.   [2] *Supra*, (4) p. 6.   [3] *Infra*, p. 179.

of Monsieur Fréart de Chambray[1], but in the reverse of his insolent way.

(6) An index of the names of authors cited, and their edition, year, etc., e.g. Junius (*Dict. de pictura veterum*, etc.), that in the body of the treatise, and even in the mere notes, or margin of the notes, (according to Mr Bayle re-iterare citations), there may be no need of more than the word Junius.

[D. NOTES.] (1) Observe in the notes under the text to speak always (without once failing) in the style of *we*, *us*, and *our*, for *I*, *me*, and *mine*. Also the author and the authors, keeping the *I* and *me* for the text : which the epistolary address may excuse.

Yet even here remember to use it as little as possible : and to substitute in its room, the fashionable *one*, from the French *on*, viz. *on solitude, on voudroit, on est bien aise*. The free use of the *ego* or *I* will be best near the beginning of each head or division, part, or chapter, where the epistolary address is renewed and fresh in the ear.

Observe also that if the Letter and Notion be first printed (as the case was with Char-cks), and afterwards the whole together under the answerable general title of Second Characters ; in this case, for better proportion's sake and uniformity of the print, many more notes may be taken into the Letter, Notion, and Emblem, and such thrown off from the last treatise, (Plasticks) as may best ease that full page, which will be still the more eased in double and triple proportion by referring from thence hither.

(2) A rule, viz. : Nothing in the text but what shall be of easy, smooth, and polite reading, without seeming difficulty, or hard study ; so that the better and gentler rank of painters and artists, the ladies, beaux, courtly gentlemen, and more refined sort of country and town wits, and notable talkers may comprehend, or be persuaded that they comprehend, what

---

[1] [Cf. Roland Fréart, Sieur de Cambray's *An idea of the Perfection of Painting*. Translated by J. Evelyn. Lond. 1668. Adv.]

is there written in the text. All besides, (viz. the Greek, Latin, Italian, and French terms of art, criticisms, and more learned remarks, or clearings, on history, nature, philosophy, and the places of Char-cks), to be reserved for notes, of which the easiest may be distinguished from the rest (as Mr Coste has done the hardest in his translated *Hiero*) by a particular kind of character or form. The notes which are to have the hands (as in paragraph (4) just above) being to pass as among the harder sort, fit only for the critic, the real virtuoso, or philosopher.

(3) In the fourth and great piece (viz. after Letter of Design, The Hercules of Prodicus, and The Appendix, or Emblem of Cebes) remember somewhere in the beginning of some chapter near the beginning of the treatise to prepare and give notice of the frequent references to the Notion, etc. : that being practical, this speculative ; that proof and fact, this descant and remark. So reference and recourse thither by citation, as to axioms or postulates, demonstrations, etc.

[E. HEADS.] (1) Not too frequent in the division of heads, e.g. The five parts in general and the five particular to be in one chapter, together with anticipation-article and ridicule of usual parallels run between the two arts[1]. All this chapter in one head.

(2) To twist, as it were, and interweave morality with plasticks, that supreme beauty with this subaltern ; those high and severe maxims with these curious and severe in their kind.

Thus the Notion and Prodicus piece, in the same original view as recited by Socrates and recorded by Xenophon (no ill-grounded design or abuse, but the stratagem and original) by the absolute opposition of pleasure to virtue, and the secret anti-Epicurean view running through the whole.

NOTE. This may be said introductorily in the beginning of some chapter and confessed pleasantly

[1] *Infra*, p. 140.

and with raillery. Though with this artifice, that in this very chapter where warning is given there should be less doctrine, depth of morals, or learning discovered, only a small show or pattern of it ; which the reader with little study may discover and applaud himself for it, believing the rest easy. So that it is in the next following chapters that the maxims, or deep precepts, theorems, etc. may be couched, and so delivered, that what surpasses the ignorant reader may pass him by, without reproaching him his defect, or frightening him with the supposed profoundness of the sense or reading.

Hence maxims[1] and citations[2] to be employed according to the heads.

(3) In this view examine and recollect sometimes in seriousness the Ἀσκήματα[3], old and new, with the chapters of the divine man, particularly what is said in the old about the τέλος, *end*, and in the new on the τὸ καλόν. Also Sensus Communis[4]. Effect of poetic (and so plastic) art, viz. and "in vocal measures of syllables and sounds, to express the harmony and numbers of an inward kind[5]." And follows next page, viz. : "that what we most admired even in the turn of outward features, was but a mysterious expression of something inward[6]" etc. Also a little below again of the same Treatise : " For all beauty is truth[7]." The τὸ εὐσύνοπτον[8], with all that follows in that remarkable virtuoso-place of maxims, which must be in part or whole copied and commented at large in Second Characters, showing the dependency of the first on second, i.e. of 'Characteristics' on this new Treatise, and *vice versa*.

[F. Citations.] (1) Citations of moderns. This work *quatenus* poetical (as plastical, pictorial), may

---

[1] *Infra*, p. 153.   [2] *Infra*, p. 170.
[3] [Cf. Shaftesbury's *Life, Letters, and Philosophical Regimen*, edited by Benjamin Rand, Lond. 1900, pp. 1–272.]
[4] Cf. Shaftesbury's *Characteristics*, Lond. 1790, I.
[5] *Ibid.* p. 137.   [6] *Ibid.* p. 138.
[7] *Ibid.* p. 142.   [8] *Ibid.* p. 143.

take in, especially in the notes, many of our best English poets in citations, the moderns who are friends for liberty, as Rowe, Congreve (though the latter too immoral in his comedy), and Dryden (with the same rebuke) for equity, and on account of his assisted translation (by my old friend Moyle, whom he names in his preface) of Virgil's two philosophical, theistical, hypothesis-passages: viz. his bees in the 'Georgics,' *Esse apibus partem divinae mentis*[1], etc.; and his Sixth 'Aeneid,' *Spiritus intus alit*[2], etc. To which if as well done by that translator add (for equity's sake also on the atheist's side) the song of Silenus[3].

N.B. Search Mr Rowe's 'Tamerlane' for any good moral lines...Also Philips'[4] 'Cyder,' the praises of honesty, etc., whom we would name with praise, but for his sottish life, gross flattery to his patrons, and consequent slavish principles. Also Lord Landsdown (when Mr Granville) not naming: his ecstasy on honesty in one of Jacob Tonson's 'Miscellany Poems.' "And what there? Take a place at court." Betray country. Be a Frenchman, anything. This last abated. No personal invective. Also a rule in this place: Not cite a prose author. Else why not preface to Au[r] of Denmark and other friends.

(2) On all occasions of citations of classic authors (the poets especially) make it a rule to consult the old editions and best commentators to make sure of the right text, orthography and interpretation. As also

---

[1] *Georgics*, IV. 220.   [2] *Aeneid*, VI. 726.

[3] The sixth pastoral in Dryden's translation of Virgil.

[4] The new Mr Philips, author of the pretty lines in the letter of the Frost from Copenhagen, and since author of a tragedy Andromache (which remember to look over together with Racine's and the ancients). Also author of pastorals, whence called "The Happy Swain." The Tragedy of Andromache is entitled "The Distresst Mother." And who seemed taken with Char-cks in letter from Sir N to my W- of 21 March 1712.

[John Philips (1679–1709) mentioned in the text wrote the 'Cyder' in imitation of Virgil's *Georgics*; and Ambrose Philips (1675?–1749) called The new' in the note wrote the 'Epistle to the Earl of Dorset,' dated Copenhagen, 9 March, 1709, as also 'Pastorals' and 'The Distresst Mother.']

to discover (what may sometimes prove very happy) the parallel places of other authors.

(3) Liberty of self-citation[1]. The use of the ego banished in all but the epistolary kind (viz. in the Inquiry and in Hercules and Cebes). "For who am I?[2]" i.e. forsooth, referring to the author's name, title, (reverend, honourable,) and picture in the front, and title-page, with the testimonial, enconiums, verses, prefacing self-adornments, and dressing. And even the *we, us, ours*, never used but in a sense[3] as it were, taking in the reader, cooperating with the writer, and discovering, investigating, as a party himself[4].

PREFATORY ANTICIPATORY THOUGHTS,
BELONGING TO EACH PIECE SEVERALLY

(1) In some of the early divisions raise the objection of luxury and expense encouraged in the great and consequently too in the little according to Esop's and Horace's Fables so unto themselves. But first a compromise, a compounding, a less for a greater and worse. A taking off from play, equipage, riot and feast, nay even from building; and in the next place when the extravagance is committed, and the *res*, the patrimony hurt, (of which speak seriously as the way to knavery, court dependence, etc. in the gentlemen), all may be retrieved, and upon a new turn of business with a good air disposed of, and with good advantage and increase of the principal, if such rules

[1] So in particular and principally in respect of the new volume of Second Characters. See Char-cks, Vol. I, viz. in Soliloquy, p. 333. Apology for present recourse to the rules of artists, painters, statuaries, the best masters, etc.

[2] This mentioned for the sake of other future authors, who may write on other kinds, and greater compositions (poem and discourse), improving still our language, and raising our ear, taste, correctness, etc.

[3] Otherwise the repeated use of *we* makes the selfishness more ridiculously, as may be easily observed in Dr Davenant, and exalts the author to the style and language of royalty.

[4] This may, in one of the after-appendices, advertisements, indexes, mentioned above, p. 7, be inserted as a remark on style, together with the other laws of correctness imposed by the author on himself.

as these are followed and not fancy. For this is worthy observation that though we scarce see a man whose fancy agrees with another in the many hands and paintings; yet in general when the Cabal is over, for this must be excepted (as in Poussin's case in France and Domenichino at Naples), the public always judges right, and the pieces esteemed or disesteemed after a time and a course of some years are always exactly esteemed according to their proportion of worth by these rules and studies, so that the gentleman who follows lies and caprice may undo himself. But he who either fixes his taste or brief according to the universal judgment and public taste and confession of painters in works of the deceased will never be abused or come off a sufferer when he parts with his effects.

In one of the exordiums or preface-addresses to my Lord *** of the earliest chapters must be represented by way of apology at being led hither insensibly by his Lordship's desire[1], the time, (the times), place, conversation, circumstance of health, and the amusements of Hercules, Cebes, etc. in paint (and thence Letter, Notion); that having formerly and at first applied only as others by mere taste not judgment or speculation, resolved (being invited to the exercise) to dissect the *je ne sais quoi*, etc.

(2) "He and he only," (upon the tone of the Moralists near the end), the *undique tutus* [everywhere secure] and recalcitrator; "He only can ridicule," and without ridicule greater on himself (as in Essay on Raillery, etc.) can despise and rally virtuosos, who is himself the great virtuoso, sage, philosopher, self-measurer, self-examiner, critic, student and pursuer of beauty, architect (as in The Moralists), plastic, inamorato, etc. (as in Moralists, not so near the end, viz. Enthusiasm vindicated) of the highest order and in the first species and primary characters. None presume to laugh at Second Characters, being not

---

[1] *Infra*, p. 23.

masters in first. This in answer to the pretended moralist, philosopher, grave censurer, and affected ignorant despiser of these studies.

(3) He who studies and breaks through the shell must see some way into the kernel. Other rules of physiognomy false; but motion of the passions and the traces which they make and leave, this true. And hence the solution of the truth whatever there is in physiognomy, except merely imbecility, idiotism, deformed organs and consequent obstructions, etc.

(4) Remember somewhere early in the explanatory parts to apologise for using painter's vulgar terms, though coarsely and improperly: but to this Horace's *usus*.

(5) And that as to painters, though not so absolutely the chief artists, not raised above statuarys, (were there any truly worthy of that name in this age, or since the ancients), yet their name always for shortness and clearness made use of for all plastic artists and their art, for all plastic art and architecture itself, as far as architecture relates to drawing and design on which indeed it fundamentally relies.

(6) Also at the very entrance apology to my Lord *** for the poetic style, alluding to what said to him in the correspondent first Letter of Enthusiasm at the beginning.

(7) Also, early, or at least in some of the first heads, declarations and raillery against affected French and Italian terms; as far as possible without affectation on the other side against what is established and has already gained[1].

(8) Also a kind of playing on the word *Second Characters*, as second parts in drama, secondary underparts. The author reduced to this, excluded the higher: content in lower, always something towards, etc., καλόν, φίλον, etc. This according to the tone of the Letter of Design[2].

---

[1] Dictionary, *infra*, p. 179   [2] *Infra*, p. 18.

Premise and distinguish between the worthy to be criticised, and the unworthy to be named. Of the former sort, (among authors), Fontenel[1], (among painters), Rubens, Le Brun, scarce a French painter besides, not reckoning Poussin[2], a naturalized Roman, really naturalized, after having been bred up there and being invited back to France and caballed against fled to Rome with detestation of his country, which made him and Salvator Rosa (as I have been assured by the old virtuosos and painters there) so good friends : the latter being a malcontent Neapolitan dissatisfied with his countrymen as his satires show. Both these by the way were honest moral men, the latter over-soured and mortal enemy of the priests, who had nothing to take advantage of against him besides the supposed familiarity he had with his woman-servant, on which account he married her.

Also Pietro da Cortona, Jordano[3], Spaniolet[4] hardly : a villain and like his work, ill usage of poor Domenichino.

Remember as a principal and pretty early apology this viz. : objection against a great man's or a philosopher's waiting upon such slight subjects as statues, pictures, etc. " For no such precedent of old." Answer : "though Plutarch, etc., not directly ; or though Pliny and Pausanias, etc., who have not written direct, were to pass as nothing ; let this be considered that the great artists (like the great generals : Xenophon, Caesar,) could write and did so *for themselves*[5]." But now on the contrary, illiterate, vulgar,

---

[1] *Infra,* p. 159.

[2] Such is the excellent Nicolo Poussin in both parts of history and perspective, and such in the latter is his Italian brother-in-law and disciple Gaspar, who borrowed of him his surname, that they are harder to be censured in their best works than even a Raphael, a Titian, or a Carache. And had the times or his own nation given encouragement to Nicolo to pursue the great, full, and true manner (not the little and false for cabinets, and to please the delicate) he had been perhaps the greatest of moderns by far.

[3] *Infra,* p. 132.　　　　[4] *Infra,* p. 133.

[5] And so needed not that other philosophers and wits should take the province.

scarce sober, and in their wits.   No liberal education,
philosophy, or learning.   Mere mechanics.   If hit
right, by example, by rote : no reason to give for it.
Hear their common talk ! " Give me nature, " says
one ; " nothing like nature."   Then porters and whores
called to sit, or wives (as Rubens') painted over and
over, dully and insipidly.   Here the Academy-genius,
and mere Academicists as now called according to
modern institution.   At this the ablest and noblest
genius of a painter laughs or spurns, and justly.   But
what says he for himself ?   " Nature is out."   " Nature
must be mended."   " Nature is poor, imperfect, short."
And what says the pedant author (Fréart[1]), and the
other writer Bosse, etc.   Forsooth : " We must not
design in perspective as we see things, but as we ought
to see them."   This is a weak aim at good sense, but
by them made mere nonsense.

Memorandum.   To premise, as an observation on
the usefulness of the treatise (modestly insinuated) the
knowledge of men and manners even in the vulgar
characters and lives of the plastics or artists, modern
as well as ancient, chiefly modern, so well remembered and told in stories, fresh and attested without
interest or design to vary, add, or impose.   And in
this respect observe "how the works and characters
of the masters correspond to their own proper and
personal characters, legible from their artificial second
characters, i.e. their works."

[1] Concerning Mon[r] Fréart de Chambray, see also and note there what
he says of Raphael, in his 'Massacre of the Innocents,' *infra*, p. 132
and p. 167.

TREATISE I

A

LETTER

CONCERNING THE

ART, or SCIENCE

O F

DESIGN

To My LORD * * * *

——————*Ante omnia Musæ.*
Virg. Georg. Lib. ii.

Printed first in the Year M.DCC.XXXII.

A

LETTER

CONCERNING

DESIGN

My Lord,

THIS letter comes to your Lordship, accompanied
with a small writing intitled A Notion: for such
alone can that piece deservedly be called, which aspires
no higher than to the forming of a project, and that too
in so vulgar a science as painting. But whatever the
subject be, if it can prove any way entertaining to you,
it will sufficiently answer my design. And if possibly
it may have that good success, I should have no ordinary
opinion of my project; since I know how hard it would
be to give your Lordship a real entertainment of any
thing which was not in some respect worthy and useful.
On this account I must, by way of prevention,
inform your Lordship, that after I had conceived my
Notion such as you see it upon paper, I was not contented with this, but fell directly to work; and by the
hand of a master-painter brought it into practice, and
formed a real design. This was not enough. I resolved
afterwards to see what effect it would have, when taken
out of mere black-and-white, into colours: and thus a
sketch was afterwards drawn. This pleased so well,
that being encouraged by the *virtuosi*, who are so
eminent in this part of the world, I resolved at last to
engage my painter in the great work. Immediately a
cloth was bespoke of a suitable dimension, and the
figures taken as big or bigger than the common life;

the subject being of the heroic kind, and requiring rather such figures as should appear above ordinary human stature.

Thus my Notion, as light as it may prove in the treatise, is become very substantial in the workmanship. The piece is still in hand; and like to continue so for some time. Otherwise the first draught or design should have accompanied the treatise; as the treatise does this letter. But the design having grown thus into a sketch, and the sketch afterwards into a picture; I thought it fit your Lordship should either see the several pieces together, or be troubled only with that which was the best; as undoubtedly the great one must prove, if the master I employ sinks not very much below himself, in this performance.

Far surely should I be, my Lord, from conceiving any vanity or pride in amusements of such an inferior kind as these; especially were they such as they may naturally at first sight appear. I pretend not here to apologize either for them, or for myself. Your Lordship however knows, I have naturally ambition enough to make me desirous of employing myself in business of a higher order: since it has been my fortune in public affairs to act often in concert with you, and in the same views, on the interest of Europe and mankind. There was a time, and that a very early one of my life, when I was not wanting to my country, in this respect. But after some years of hearty labour and pains in this kind of workmanship, an unhappy breach in my health drove me not only from the seat of business, but forced me to seek these foreign climates; where, as mild as the winters generally are, I have with much ado lived out this latter one; and am now, as your Lordship finds, employing myself in such easy studies as are most suitable to my state of health, and to the genius of the country where I am confined.

This in the meantime I can, with some assurance say to your Lordship in a kind of spirit of prophecy, from what I have observed of the rising genius of our nation, That if we live to see a peace any way answerable to that generous spirit with which this war was begun, and carried on, for our own liberty and that of Europe; the figure we are like to make abroad, and the increase of knowledge, industry and sense at home, will render united Britain the principal seat of arts; and by her politeness and advantages in this kind, will shew evidently, how much she owes to those counsels, which taught her to exert herself so resolutely on behalf of the common cause, and that of her own liberty, and happy constitution, necessarily included.

I can myself remember the time, when, in respect of music, our reigning taste was in many degrees inferior to the French. The long reign of luxury and pleasure under King Charles the Second, and the foreign helps and studied advantages given to music in a following reign, could not raise our genius the least in this respect. But when the spirit of the nation was grown more free, though engaged at that time in the fiercest war, and with the most doubtful success, we no sooner began to turn ourselves towards music, and enquire what Italy in particular produced, than in an instant we outstripped our neighbours the French, entered into a genius far beyond theirs, and raised ourselves an ear, and judgment, not inferior to the best now in the world.

In the same manner, as to painting. Though we have as yet nothing of our own native growth in this kind worthy of being mentioned; yet since the public has of late begun to express a relish for engravings, drawings, copyings, and for the original paintings of the chief Italian schools (so contrary to the modern French), I doubt not that, in very few years we shall make an equal progress in this other science. And when our humour turns us to cultivate these designing arts, our genius, I am persuaded, will naturally carry us over the slighter amusements, and lead us to that higher, more serious, and noble part of imitation, which relates to history, human nature, and the chief degree or order of beauty; I mean that of the rational life, distinct from the merely vegetable and sensible, as in animals, or plants; according to those several degrees or orders of painting, which your Lordship will find suggested in this extemporary Notion I have sent you.

As for architecture, it is no wonder if so many noble designs of this kind have miscarried amongst us; since the genius of our nation has hitherto been so little turned this way, that through several reigns we have patiently seen the noblest public buildings perish (if I may say so) under the hand of one single court-architect; who, if he had been able to profit by experience, would long since, at our expense, have proved the greatest master in the world. But I question whether our patience is like to hold much longer. The devastation so long committed in this kind, has made us begin to grow rude and clamorous at the hearing of a new palace spoilt, or a new design committed to some rash or impotent pretender.

It is the good fate of our nation in this particular, that there remain yet two of the noblest subjects for architecture; our Prince's Palace and our House of Parliament. For I cannot but fancy that when Whitehall is thought of, the neighbouring Lords and Commons will at the same time be placed in better chambers and apartments, than at present; were it only for majesty's sake, and as a magnificence becoming the person of the Prince, who here appears in full solemnity. Nor do I fear that when these new subjects are attempted, we should miscarry as grossly as we have done in others before. Our State, in this respect, may prove perhaps more fortunate than our Church, in having waited till a national taste was formed, before these edifices were undertaken. But the zeal of the nation could not, it seems, admit so long a delay in their ecclesiastical structures, particularly their metropolitan. And since a zeal of this sort has been newly kindled amongst us, it is like we shall see from afar the many spires arising in our great city, with such hasty and sudden growth, as may be the occasion perhaps that our immediate relish shall be hereafter censured, as retaining much of what artists call the Gothic kind.

Hardly, indeed, as the public now stands, should we bear to see a Whitehall treated like a Hampton Court, or even a new cathedral like St Paul's. Almost every one now becomes concerned, and interests himself in such public structures. Even those pieces too are brought under the common censure, which, though raised by private men, are of such a grandeur and magnificence, as to become national ornaments. The ordinary man may build his cottage, or the plain gentleman his country house according as he fancies: but when a great man builds, he will find little quarter from the public, if instead of a beautiful pile, he raises, at a vast expense, such a false and counterfeit piece of magnificence, as can be justly arraigned for its deformity by so many knowing men in art, and by the whole people, who, in such a conjuncture readily follow their opinion.

In reality the people are no small parties in this cause. Nothing moves successfully without them. There can be no public, but where they are included. And without a public voice, knowingly guided and directed, there is nothing which can raise a true ambition in the artist; nothing which can exalt the genius of the workman, or make him emulous of after fame, and of the approbation of his country, and of posterity. For with these he naturally, as a freeman, must take part: in these he has a passionate concern, and interest, raised in him by the same genius of liberty, the same laws and government, by which his property and the rewards of his pains and industry, are secured to him, and to his generation after him.

Everything co-operates, in such a State, towards the improvement of art and science. And for the designing arts in particular, such as architecture, painting, and statuary, they are in a manner linked together. The taste of one kind brings necessarily that of the others along with it. When the free spirit of a nation turns itself this way, judgments are formed; critics arise; the public eye and ear improve; a right taste prevails, and in a manner forces its way. Nothing is so improving, nothing so natural, so congenial to the liberal arts, as that reigning liberty and high spirit of a people, which from the habit of judging in the highest matters for themselves, makes them freely judge of other subjects, and enter thoroughly into the characters as well of men and manners, as of the products or works of men, in art and science. So much, my Lord, do we owe to the excellence of our national constitution, and legal monarchy; happily fitted for us, and which alone could hold together so mighty a people; all sharers (though at so far a distance from each other) in the government of themselves; and meeting under one head in one vast metropolis; whose enormous growth, however censurable in other respects, is actually a cause that workmanship and arts of so many kinds arise to such perfection.

What encouragement our higher powers may think fit to give these growing arts, I will not pretend to guess. This I know, that it is so much for their advantage and interest to make themselves the chief parties in the cause, that I wish no court or ministry, besides a truly virtuous and wise one, may ever concern themselves in the affair. For should they do so, they would in reality do more harm than good; since it is not the nature of a court (such as courts generally are) to improve, but rather corrupt a taste. And what is in the beginning set wrong by their example, is hardly ever afterwards recoverable in the genius of a nation.

Content therefore I am, my Lord, that Britain stands in this respect as she now does. Nor can one, methinks, with just reason regret her having hitherto made no greater advancement in these affairs of art. As her constitution has grown, and been established, she has in proportion fitted herself for other improvements. There has been no anticipation in the case. And in this surely she must be esteemed wise, as well as happy; that ere she attempted to raise herself any other taste or relish, she secured herself a right one in government. She has now the advantage of beginning in other matters on a new foot. She has her models yet to seek, her scale and standard to form, with deliberation and good choice. Able enough she is at present to shift for herself; however abandoned or helpless she has been left by those whom it became to assist her. Hardly, indeed, could she procure a single academy for the training of her youth in exercises. As good soldiers as we are, and as good horses as our climate affords, our Princes, rather than expend their treasure this way, have suffered our youth to pass into a foreign nation, to learn to ride. As for other academies, such as those for painting, sculpture, or architecture, we have not so much as heard of the proposal; whilst the Prince of our rival nation raises academies, breeds youth, and sends rewards and pensions into foreign countries, to advance the interest and credit of his own. Now if, notwithstanding the industry and pains of this foreign court, and the supine unconcernedness of our own, the national taste however rises, and already shews itself in many respects beyond that of our so highly assisted neighbours; what greater proof can there be of the superiority of genius in one of these nations above the other?

It is but this moment that I chance to read in an article of one of the gazettes from Paris, that it is resolved at court to establish a new academy for political affairs. "In it the present chief minister is to preside; having under him six academists, *douëz des talens nécessaires.*—No person to be received under the age of twenty-five. A thousand livres pension for each scholar.—Able masters to be appointed for teaching them the necessary sciences, and instructing them in the Treaties of Peace and Alliances, which have been formerly made.—The members to assemble three times a week.—*C'est de ce Seminaire* (says the writer) *qu'on tirera les secretaires d'Ambassade; qui par degrez pourront monter à de plus hauts emplois.*"

I must confess, my Lord, as great an admirer as I am of these regular institutions, I cannot but look upon an academy for ministers as a very extraordinary establishment; especially in such a monarchy as France, and at such a conjuncture as the present. It looks as if the ministers of that court had discovered lately some new methods of negotiation, such as their predecessors Richelieu and Mazarine never thought of; or that, on the contrary, they have found themselves so declined, and at such a loss in the management of this present treaty, as to be forced to take their lesson from some of those ministers with whom they treat: a reproach, of which, no doubt, they must be highly sensible.

But it is not my design here, to entertain your Lordship with any reflections upon politics, or the methods which the French may take to raise themselves new ministers, or new generals; who may prove a better match for us than hitherto, whilst we held our old. I will only say to your Lordship on this subject of academies; that indeed I have less concern for the deficiency of such a one as this, than of any other which could be thought of, for England; and that as for a seminary of statesmen, I doubt not but, without this extraordinary help, we shall be able, out of our old stock, and the common course of business, constantly to furnish a sufficient number of well qualified persons to serve upon occasion, either at home, or in our foreign treaties; as often as such persons accordingly qualified shall duly, honestly, and *bona fide* be required to serve.

I return therefore to my *virtuoso* science; which being my chief amusement in this place and circumstance, your Lordship has by it a fresh instance that I can never employ my thoughts with satisfaction on any subject, without making you a party. For even this very notion had its rise chiefly from the conversation of a certain day, which I had the happiness to pass a few years since in the country with your Lordship.

It was there you shewed me some engravings, which had been sent you from Italy. One in particular I well remember; of which the subject was the very same with that of my written Notion enclosed. But by what hand it was done, or after what master, or how executed, I have quite forgot. It was the summer season, when you had recess from business. And I have accordingly calculated this epistle and project for the same recess and leisure. For by the time this can reach England, the spring will be far advanced, and the national affairs in a manner over, with those who are not in the immediate administration.

Were that indeed your Lordship's lot, at present; I know not whether in regard to my country I should dare throw such amusements as these in your way. Yet even in this case, I would venture to say however, in defence of my project, and of the cause of painting; that could my young hero come to your Lordship as well represented as he might have been, either by the hand of a Marat[1] or a Jordano (the masters who were in being, and in repute, when I first travelled here in Italy), the picture itself, whatever the treatise proved, would have been worth notice, and might have become a present worthy of our court and Prince's palace; especially were it so blessed as to lodge within it a royal issue of her Majesty's. Such a piece of furniture might well fit the gallery, or hall of exercises, where our young Princes should learn their usual lessons. And to see virtue in this garb and action, might perhaps be no slight memorandum hereafter to a royal youth, who should one day come to undergo this trial himself; on which his own happiness, as well as the fate of Europe and of the world, would in so great a measure depend.

This, my Lord, is making (as you see) the most I can of my project, and setting off my amusements

---

[1] Carlo Marat was yet alive at the time when this letter was written; but had long been superannuated, and incapable of any considerable performance.

with the best colour I am able; that I may be the more excusable in communicating them to your Lordship, and expressing thus, with what zeal I am,

My Lord,

Your Lordship's

most faithful humble Servant,

SHAFTESBURY.

NAPLES, *March* 6.
N. S. 1712.

TREATISE II

A NOTION of the *Historical Draught* or *Tablature*

OF THE

JUDGMENT of *HERCULES*

According to PRODICUS, *Lib*. II. *Xen. de Mem. Soc.*

—————————————————Potiores
HERCULIS ærumnas credat, sævosque labores,
Et Venere, et cœnis, et pluma SARDANAPALI.

Juv. Sat. 10.

Printed first in English in the Year M.DCC.XIII.

Paulo de Matthæis Pinx Sim. Gribelin Sculps:

A NOTION

OF THE

HISTORICAL DRAUGHT

OF

HERCULES[1]

INTRODUCTION

(1) BEFORE we enter on the examination of our historical sketch, it may be proper to remark, that by the word Tablature (for which we have yet no name in English, besides the general one of picture) we

[1] [In order that the reader may better understand this discussion it is necessary to have before the mind the principal circumstances of the choice of Hercules as uttered by the Sophist Prodicus and related by Xenophon in the *Memorabilia*, II. I. 21. " Prodicus the sophist, also, in his

denote, according to the original word Tabula, a work not only distinct from a mere portraiture, but from all those wilder sorts of painting which are in a manner narrative concerning Hercules, which he indeed declaims to most people as a specimen of his ability, expresses a similar notion respecting virtue, speaking, as far as I remember, to the following effect: For he says that Hercules, when he was advancing from boyhood to manhood, a period at which the young, becoming their own masters, begin to give intimations whether they will enter on life by the path of virtue or that of vice, went forth into a solitary place, and sat down, perplexed as to which of these two paths he should pursue; 22. and that two female figures, of lofty stature, seemed to advance toward him, the one of an engaging and graceful mien, gifted by nature with elegance of form, modesty of look, and sobriety of demeanour, and clad in a white robe; the other fed to plumpness and softness, but assisted by art both in her complexion, so as to seem fairer and rosier than she really was, and in her gesture, so as to seem taller than her natural height; she had her eyes wide open, and a robe through which her beauty would readily show itself; she frequently contemplated her figure, and looked about to see if any one else was observing her; and she frequently glanced back at her own shadow. 23. As they approached near to Hercules, she, whom I first described, came forward at the same pace, but the other, eager to get before her, ran up to Hercules, and exclaimed, "I see that you are hesitating, Hercules, by what path you shall enter upon life; if then you make a friend of me, I will conduct you by the most delightful and easy road, you shall taste of every species of pleasure, and lead a life free from every sort of trouble..."

26. Hercules, on hearing this address, said, "And what, O woman, is your name?" "My friends," she replied, "call me Happiness, but those who hate me, give me, to my disparagement, the name of Vice."

27. In the meantime the other female approached, and said, "I also am come to address you, Hercules, because I know your parents, and have observed your disposition in the training of your childhood, from which I entertain hopes, that if you direct your steps along the path that leads to my dwelling, you will become an excellent performer of whatever is honourable and noble, and that I shall appear more honourable and attractive through your illustrious deeds. I will not deceive you, however, with promises of pleasure, but will set before you things as they really are, and as the gods have appointed them; 28. for of what is valuable and excellent the gods grant nothing to mankind without labour and care; and if you wish the gods, therefore, to be propitious to you, you must worship the gods; if you seek to be loved by your friends, you must serve your friends; if you desire to be honoured by any city, you must benefit that city; if you long to be admired by all Greece for your merit, you must endeavour to be of advantage to all Greece; if you are anxious that the earth should yield you abundance of fruit, you must cultivate the earth; if you think that you should enrich yourself from herds of cattle, you must bestow care upon herds of cattle; if you are eager to increase your means by war, and to secure freedom to your friends and subdue your enemies, you must learn the arts of war, and learn them from such as understand them, and practice how to use them with advantage; if you wish to be vigorous in body, you must accustom your body to obey your mind, and exercise it with toil and exertion."

Here Vice, interrupting her speech, said, (as Prodicus relates,) " Do

absolute, and independent; such as the paintings in fresco upon the walls, the ceilings, the staircases, the cupola's, and other remarkable places either of churches or palaces.

(2) Accordingly we are to understand, that it is not merely the shape or dimension of a cloth, or board, which denominates the piece or tablature; since a work of this kind may be composed of any coloured substance, as it may of any form; whether square, oval or round. But it is then that in painting we may give to any particular work the name of Tablature, when the work is in reality "a single piece, comprehended in one view, and formed according to one single intelligence, meaning, or design; which constitutes a real whole, by a mutual and necessary relation of its parts, the same as of the members in a natural body." So that one may say of a picture composed of any number of figures differently ranged, and without any regard to this correspondency or union described, that it is no more a real piece or tablature than a picture would be a man's picture, or proper portraiture, which represented

you see Hercules, by how difficult and tedious a road this woman conducts you to gratification, while I shall lead you by an easy and short path to perfect happiness?"

"Wretched being," rejoined Virtue, "of what good are you in possession? Or what real pleasure do you experience, when you are unwilling to do anything for the attainment of it?"...32. But I am the companion of the gods; I associate with virtuous men; no honourable deed, divine or human, is done without me; I am honoured most of all by the deities, and by those among men to whom it belongs to honour me, being a welcome co-operator with artisans, a faithful household guardian to masters, a benevolent assistant to servants, a benign promoter of the labours of peace, a constant auxiliary to the efforts of war, an excellent sharer in friendship.   33. My friends have a sweet and untroubled enjoyment of meat and drink, for they refrain from them till they feel an appetite. They have also sweeter sleep than the idle; and are neither annoyed if they lose a portion of it, nor neglect to do their duties for the sake of it. The young are pleased with praises from the old; the old are delighted with honours from the young. They remember their former acts with pleasure, and rejoice to perform their present occupations with success; being through my influence, dear to the gods, beloved by their friends, and honoured by their country. And when the destined end of life comes, they do not lie in oblivion and dishonour, but, celebrated with songs and praise, flourish for ever in the memory of mankind. By such a course of conduct, O Hercules, son of noble parents, you may secure the most exalted happiness." Bohn's ed.]

on the same cloth, in different places, the legs, arms, nose, and eyes of such a person, without adjusting them according to the true proportion, air, and character which belonged to him.

(3) This regulation has place even in the inferior degrees of painting; since the mere flower-painter is, we see, obliged to study the form of festoons and to make use of a peculiar order, or architecture of vases, jars, cannisters, pedestals, and other inventions, which serve as machines, to frame a certain proportionate assemblage, or united mass, according to the rules of perspective; and with regard as well to the different shapes and sizes of his several flowers, as to the harmony of colours resulting from the whole: this being the only thing capable of rendering his work worthy the name of a composition or real piece.

(4) So much the more, therefore, is this regulation applicable to history-painting, where not only men, but manners, and human passions are represented. Here the unity of design must with more particular exactness be preserved, according to the just rules of poetic art; that in the representation of any event, or remarkable fact, the probability, or seeming truth (which is the real truth of art) may with the highest advantage be supported and advanced: as we shall better understand in the argument which follows on the historical tablature of the Judgment of Hercules; who being young, and retired to a solitary place in order to deliberate on the choice he was to make of the different ways of life, was accosted (as our historian relates) by the two goddesses, Virtue and Pleasure. It is on the issue of the controversy between these two, that the character of Hercules depends. So that we may naturally give to this piece and history, as well the title of The Education, as the Choice or Judgment of Hercules.

CHAPTER I

OF THE GENERAL CONSTITUTION OR ORDINANCE
OF THE TABLATURE

(1) THIS fable or history may be variously represented, according to the order of time:

Either in the instant when the two goddesses (Virtue and Pleasure) accost Hercules;

Or when they are entered on their dispute;

Or when their dispute is already far advanced, and Virtue seems to gain her cause.

(2) According to the first notion, Hercules must of necessity seem surprized on the first appearance of such miraculous forms.   He admires, he contemplates; but is not yet engaged or interested.   According to the second notion, he is interested, divided, and in doubt.   According to the third, he is wrought, agitated, and torn by contrary passions.   It is the last effort of the virtuous one, striving for possession over him.   He agonizes, and with all his strength of reason endeavours to overcome himself:

Et premitur ratione animus, vincique laborat.

(3) Of these different periods of time, the latter has been chosen; as being the only one of the three, which can well serve to express the grand event, or consequent resolution of Hercules, and the choice he actually made of a life full of toil and hardship, under the conduct of Virtue, for the deliverance of mankind from tyranny and oppression.   And it is to such a piece, or tablature, as represents this issue of the

balance, in our pondering hero, that we may justly give the title of the Decision or Judgment of Hercules.

(4) The same history may be represented yet according to a fourth date or period: as at the time when Hercules is entirely won by Virtue. But then the signs of this resolute determination reigning absolutely in the attitude, and air of our young hero; there would be no room left to represent his agony, or inward conflict, which indeed makes the principal action here; as it would do in a poem, were this subject to be treated by a good poet. Nor would there be any more room left in this case, either for the persuasive rhetoric of Virtue (who must have already ended her discourse) or for the insinuating address of Pleasure, who having lost her cause, must necessarily appear displeased, or out of humour: a circumstance which would no way suit her character.

(5) In the original story or fable of this adventure of our young Hercules, it is particularly noted, that Pleasure, advancing hastily before Virtue, began her plea, and was heard with prevention; as being first in turn. And as this fable is wholly philosophical and moral, this circumstance in particular is to be considered as essential.

(6) In this third period therefore of our history (dividing it, as we have done, into four successive dates or points of time) Hercules being auditor, and attentive, speaks not. Pleasure has spoken. Virtue is still speaking. She is about the middle, or towards the end of her discourse; in the place where, according to just rhetoric, the highest tone of voice and strongest action are employed.

(7) It is evident, that every master in painting, when he has made choice of the determinate date or point of time, according to which he would represent his history, is afterwards debarred the taking advantage from any other action than what is immediately present, and belonging to that single instant he describes. For if he passes the present only for a moment, he may as

well pass it for many years. And by this reckoning
he may with as good right repeat the same figure
several times over, and in one and the same picture
represent Hercules in his cradle, struggling with the
serpents; and the same Hercules of full age, fighting
with the Hydra, with Anteus, and with Cerberus:
which would prove a mere confused heap, or knot of
pieces, and not a single entire piece, or tablature, of the
historical kind.

(8) It may however be allowable, on some
occasions, to make use of certain enigmatical or
emblematical devices, to represent a future time: as
when Hercules, yet a mere boy, is seen holding a
small club, or wearing the skin of a young lion. For
so we often find him in the best antiques. And though
history had never related of Hercules, that being yet
very young, he killed a lion with his own hand; this
representation of him would nevertheless be entirely
conformable to poetic truth; which not only admits,
but necessarily presupposes prophecy or prognostica-
tion, with regard to the actions, and lives of heroes
and great men. Besides that as to our subject, in
particular, the natural genius of Hercules, even in his
tenderest youth, might alone answer for his handling
such arms as these, and bearing, as it were in play,
these early tokens of the future hero.

(9) To preserve therefore a just conformity with
historical truth, and with the unity of time and action,
there remains no other way by which we can possibly
give a hint of any thing future, or call to mind any thing
past, than by setting in view such passages or events
as have actually subsisted, or according to nature might
well subsist, or happen together in one and the same
instant. And this is what we may properly call the
rule of consistency.

(10) How is it therefore possible, says one, to
express a change of passion in any subject, since this
change is made by succession; and that in this case
the passion which is understood as present, will require

a disposition of body and features wholly different from the passion which is over, and past? To this we answer, That notwithstanding the ascendency or reign of the principal and immediate passion, the artist has power to leave still in his subject the tracts or footsteps of its predecessor: so as to let us behold not only a rising passion together with a declining one; but, what is more, a strong and determinate passion, with its contrary already discharged and banished. As for instance, when the plain tracts of tears new fallen, with other fresh tokens of mourning and dejection, remain still in a person newly transported with joy at the sight of a relation or friend, who the moment before had been lamented as one deceased or lost.

(11) Again, by the same means which are employed to call to mind the past, we may anticipate the future: as would be seen in the case of an able painter, who should undertake to paint this history of Hercules according to the third date or period of time proposed for our historical tablature. For in this momentary turn of action, Hercules remaining still in a situation expressive of suspense and doubt, would discover nevertheless that the strength of this inward conflict was over, and that victory began now to declare herself in favour of virtue. This transition, which seems at first so mysterious a performance, will be easily comprehended, if one considers, that the body, which moves much slower than the mind, is easily outstripped by this latter; and that the mind on a sudden turning itself some new way, the nearer situated and more sprightly parts of the body (such as the eyes, and muscles about the mouth and forehead) taking the alarm, and moving in an instant, may leave the heavier and more distant parts to adjust themselves, and change their attitude some moments after.

(12) This different operation may be distinguished by the names of anticipation and repeal.

(13) If by any other method an artist should

pretend to introduce into this piece any portion of time, future or past, he must either sin directly against the law of truth and credibility, in representing things contrary and incompatible; or against that law of unity and simplicity of design, which constitutes the very being of his work. This particularly shews itself in a picture, when one is necessarily left in doubt, and unable to determine readily, which of the distinct successive parts of the history or action is that very one represented in the design. For even here the case is the same as in the other circumstances of poetry and painting: "That what is principal or chief, should immediately shew itself, without leaving the mind in any uncertainty."

(14) According to this rule of the unity of time, if one should ask an artist, who had painted this history of the Judgment of Hercules, "Which of these four periods or dates of time above proposed he intended in his picture to represent[1]?" and it should happen that he could not readily answer, It was this, or that: it would appear plainly he had never formed a real notion of his workmanship, or of the history he intended to represent. So that when he had executed even to a miracle all those other beauties requisite in a piece, and had failed in this single one, he would from hence alone be proved to be in truth no history-painter, or artist in the kind, who understood not so much as how to form the real design of a historical piece.

[1] If the same question concerning the instantaneous action, or present moment of time, were applied to many famous historical paintings much admired in the world, they would be found very defective: as we may learn by the instance of that single subject of Acteon, one of the commonest in painting. Hardly is there anywhere seen a design of this poetical history, without a ridiculous anticipation of the metamorphosis. The horns of Acteon, which are the effect of a charm, should naturally wait the execution of that act in which the charm consists. Till the goddess therefore has thrown her cast, the hero's person suffers not any change. Even while the water flies, his forehead is still found. But in the usual design we see it otherwise. The horns are already sprouted, if not full grown: and the goddess is seen watering the sprouts.

CHAPTER II

(1) To apply therefore what has been said above to our immediate design or tablature in hand; we may observe, in the first place, with regard to Hercules (the first or principal figure of our piece) that being placed in the middle, between the two goddesses, he should by a skilful master be so drawn, as even setting aside the air and features of the face, it should appear by the very turn or position of the body alone, that this young hero had not wholly quitted the balancing or pondering part. For in the manner of his turn towards the worthier of these goddesses, he should by no means appear so averse or separate from the other, as not to suffer it to be conceived of him, that he had ever any inclination for her, or had ever hearkened to her voice. On the contrary, there ought to be some hopes yet remaining for this latter goddess Pleasure, and some regret apparent in Hercules. Otherwise we should pass immediately from the third to the fourth period; or at least confound one with the other.

(2) Hercules, in this agony described, may appear either sitting, or standing: though it be more according to probability for him to appear standing, in regard to the presence of the two goddesses, and by reason the case is far from being the same here as in the Judgment of Paris, where the interested goddesses plead their cause before their judge. Here the interest of Hercules himself is at stake. It is his own cause which is trying. He is in this respect not so much the judge, as he is in reality the party judged.

(3) The superior and commanding passion of Hercules may be expressed either by a strong admiration, or by an admiration which holds chiefly of love.

—Ingenti perculsus amore.

(4) If the latter be used, then the reluctant passion, which is not yet wholly overcome, may shew itself in pity and tenderness, moved in our hero by the thought of those pleasures and companions of his youth, which he is going for ever to abandon. And in this sense Hercules may look either on the one or the other of the goddesses, with this difference; that if he looks on Pleasure, it should be faintly, and as turning his eyes back with pity; having still his action and gesture turned the other way towards Virtue. If, on the contrary, he looks on Virtue; it ought to be earnestly, and with extreme attention, having some part of the action of his body inclining still towards Pleasure, and discovering by certain features of concern and pity, intermixed with the commanding or conquering passion, that the decision he is about to make in favour of Virtue, cost him not a little.

(5) If it be thought fit rather to make use of admiration, merely to express the commanding passion of Hercules: then the reluctant one may discover itself in a kind of horror, at the thought of the toil and labour, to be sustained in the rough rocky way apparent on the side of Virtue.

(6) Again, Hercules may be represented as looking neither towards Virtue nor Pleasure, but as turning his eyes either towards the mountainous rocky way pointed out to him by Virtue, or towards the flowery way of the vale and meadows, recommended to him by Pleasure. And to these different attitudes for the expression of the turn or balance of judgment in our pensive hero.

(7) Whatever may be the manner chosen for the designing of this figure of Hercules, according to that part of the history in which we have taken him; it is certain he should be so drawn, as neither by the opening

of his mouth, or by any other sign, to leave it in the least dubious whether he is speaking or silent. For it is absolutely requisite that silence should be distinctly characterised in Hercules, not only as the natural effect of his strict attention, and the little leisure he has from what passes at this time within his breast; but in order withal to give that appearance of majesty and superiority becoming the person and character of pleading Virtue; who by her eloquence and other charms has ere this made herself mistress of the heart of our enamoured hero:

—*Pendetque iterum narrantis ab ore*[1].

This image of the sublime in the discourse and manner of Virtue, would be utterly lost, if in the instant that she employed the greatest force of action, she should appear to be interrupted by the ill-timed speech, reply, or utterance of her auditor. Such a design or representation as this, would prove contrary to order, contrary to the history, and to the decorum, or decency of manners. Nor can one well avoid taking notice here of that general absurdity committed by many of the esteemed great masters in painting; who in one and the same company, or assembly of persons jointly employed, and united according to the history, in one single or common action, represent to us not only two or three, but several, and sometimes all speaking at once : which must naturally have the same effect on the eye, as such a conversation would have upon the ear were we in reality to hear it.

[1] Virg. *Aen.* Lib. 4, ver. 79.

CHAPTER III

OF THE SECOND FIGURE

(1) AFTER what has been said on the subject of Hercules, it appears plainly what the attitude must be of our second figure, Virtue; who, as we have taken her in this particular period of our history, must of necessity be speaking with all the force of action, such as would appear in an excellent orator, when at the height, and in the most affecting part of his discourse.

(2) She ought therefore to be drawn standing; since it is contrary to all probable appearance, and even to nature itself, that in the very heat and highest transport of speech, the speaker should be seen sitting, or in any posture which might express repose.

(3) She may be habited either as an Amazon, with the helmet, lance, and in the robe or vest of Pallas; or as any other of the virtues, goddesses, or heroines, with the plain original crown, without rays, according to genuine antiquity. Our history makes no mention of a helmet, or any other armour of Virtue. It gives us only to understand that she was dressed neither negligently, nor with much study or ornament. If we follow this latter method, we need give her only in her hand the imperial or magisterial sword[1]; which is her true characteristic mark, and would sufficiently distinguish her, without the helmet, lance, or other military habit. And in this manner the opposition between herself and her rival would be still more beautiful and regular. —"But this beauty," says one, "would be discoverable only by the learned."—Perhaps so. But then again

---

[1] Parazonium.

there would be no loss for others: since no one would find this piece the less intelligible on the account of this regulation. On the contrary, one who chanced to know little of antiquity in general, or of this history in particular, would be still further to seek, if upon seeing an armed woman in the piece, he should represent to himself either a Pallas, a Bellona, or any other warlike form, or deity of the female kind.

(4) As for the shape, countenance, or person of Virtue; that which is usually given to Pallas may fitly serve as a model for this dame; as on the other side, that which is given to Venus may serve in the same manner for her rival. The historian whom we follow, represents Virtue to us as a lady of a goodly form, tall and majestic. And by what he relates of her, he gives us sufficiently to understand, that though she was neither lean, nor of a tanned complexion, she must have discovered however, by the substance and colour of her flesh, that she was sufficiently accustomed to exercise. Pleasure, on the other hand, by an exact opposition, is represented in better case, and of a softness of complexion; which speaks her manners, and gives her a middle character between the person of a Venus, and that of a Bacchinal nymph.

(5) As for the position, or attitude of Virtue; though in a historical piece, such as ours is designed, it would on no account be proper to have immediate recourse to the way of emblem; one might, on this occasion, endeavour nevertheless by some artifice, to give our figure, as much as possible, the resemblance of the same goddess, as she is seen on medals, and other ancient emblematic pieces of like nature. In this view, she should be so designed, as to stand firm with her full poise upon one foot, having the other a little advanced, and raised on a broken piece of ground or rock, instead of the helmet or little globe on which we see her usually setting her foot, as triumphant, in those pieces of the emblematic kind. A particular advantage of this attitude, so judiciously assigned to

Virtue by ancient masters, is, that it expresses as well her aspiring effort, or ascent towards the Stars and Heaven, as her victory and superiority over fortune and the world. For so the poets have of old described her.

—*Negata tentat iter via*[1].
Virtutisque viam deserit arduae[2].

And in our piece particularly, where the arduous and rocky way of Virtue requires to be emphatically represented; the ascending posture of this figure, with one foot advanced, in a sort of climbing action, over the rough and thorny ground, must of necessity, if well executed, create a due effect, and add to the sublime of this ancient poetic work[3].

(6) As for the hands or arms, which in real oratory, and during the strength of elocution, must of necessity be active; it is plain in respect of our goddess, that the arm in particular which she has free to herself, and is neither encumbered with lance or sword, should be employed another way, and come in, to second the discourse, and accompany it, with a just emphasis and action. Accordingly, Virtue would then be seen with this hand, turned either upwards to the rocky way marked out by her with approbation; or to the sky, or stars, in the same sublime sense; or downwards to the flowery way and vale, as in a detesting manner, and with abhorrence of what passes there; or last of all (in a disdainful sense, and with the same appearance of detestation) against Pleasure herself. Each manner would have its peculiar advantage. And the best profit

---

[1] Horat. Lib. 3, Od. 2.   [2] *Idem ibid.* Od. 24.

[3] As ancient as the poet Hesiod, which appears by the following verses, cited by our historian, as the foundation, or first draught of this Herculean tablature.

τὴν μὲν γὰρ κακότητα καὶ ἰλαδόν ἐστιν ἑλέσθαι
ῥηιδίως. λείη μὲν ὁδός, μάλα δ' ἐγγύθι ναίει·
τῆς δ' ἀρετῆς ἱδρῶτα θεοὶ προπάροιθεν ἔθηκαν
ἀθάνατοι· μακρὸς δὲ καὶ ὄρθιος οἶμος ἐπ' αὐτήν,
καὶ τρηχὺς τὸ πρῶτον· ἐπὴν δ' εἰς ἄκρον ἵκηται
ῥηιδίη δ' ἤπειτα πέλει, χαλεπή περ ἐοῦσα.

should be made of this arm and hand at liberty to express either the disapprobation or the applause proposed. It might prove, however, a considerable advantage to our figure of Virtue, if holding the lance, or imperial sword, slightly, with one of her hands stretched downwards, she could, by that very hand and action, be made to express the latter meaning; opening for that purpose some of the lower fingers of this hand, in a refusing or repelling manner; whilst with the other arm and hand at liberty, she should express as well the former meaning, and point out to Hercules the way which leads to honour, and the just glory of heroic actions.

(7) From all these circumstances of history, and action, accompanying this important figure, the difficulty of the design will sufficiently appear, to those who carry their judgment beyond the mere form, and are able to consider the character of the passion to which it is subjected. For where a real character is marked, and the inward form peculiarly described, it is necessary the outward should give place. Whoever should expect to see our figure of Virtue, in the exact mein of a fine talker, curious in her choice of action, and forming it according to the usual decorum, and regular movement of one of the fair ladies of our age, would certainly be far wide of the thought and genius of this piece. Such studied action and artificial gesture may be allowed to the actors and actresses of the stage. But the good painter must come a little nearer to truth, and take care that his action be not theatrical, or at second hand; but original, and drawn from nature herself. Now although in the ordinary tenour of discourse, the action of the party might be allowed to appear so far governed and composed by art, as to retain that regular contrast and nice balance of movement which painters are apt to admire as the chief grace of figures; yet in this particular case, where the natural eagerness of debate, supported by a thorough antipathy and animosity, is joined to a sort of

enthusiastic agitation incident to our prophetic dame, there can be little of that fashionable mien, or genteel air admitted. The painter who, in such a piece as we describe, is bound to preserve the heroic style, will doubtless beware of representing his heroine as a mere scold. Yet this is certain, that it were better for him to expose himself to the meanness of such a fancy, and paint his lady in a high rant, according to the common weakness of the sex, than to engage in the embellishment of the mere form; and forgetting the character of severity and reprimand belonging to the illustrious rival, present her to us a fair specious personage, free of emotion, and without the least bent or movement which should express the real pathetic of the kind.

CHAPTER IV

(1) CONCERNING Pleasure there needs little to be said, after what has been already remarked in relation to the two preceding figures. The truth of appearance, that of history, and even the decorum itself (according to what has been explained above) require evidently, that in this period or instant described, Pleasure should be found silent. She can have no other language allowed her than that merely of the eyes. And it would be a happy management for her in the design, if in turning her eyes to meet those of Hercules, she should find his head and face already turned so much on the contrary side, as to shew it impossible for her as yet to discover the growing passion of this hero in favour of her rival. By this means she might still with good right retain her fond airs of dalliance and court-ship; as having yet discovered no reason she has to be dissatisfied.

(2) She may be drawn either standing, leaning, sitting, or lying; without a crown, or crowned either with roses, or with myrtle; according to the painter's fancy. And since in this third figure the painter has so great a liberty left him, he may make good advantage of it for the other two, to which this latter may be subjected, as the last in order, and of least consequence.

(3) That which makes the greatest difficulty in the disposition or ordinance of this figure Pleasure, is, that notwithstanding the supine air and character of ease and indolence, which should be given her, she must retain still so much life and action, as is sufficient

to express her persuasive effort, and manner of indica-
tion towards her proper paths; those of the flowery
kind, and vale below, whither she would willingly guide
our hero's steps.   Now should this effort be over-
strongly expressed; not only the supine character and
air of indolence would be lost in this figure of Pleasure;
but, what is worse, the figure would seem to speak, or
at least appear so, as to create a double meaning, or
equivocal sense in painting; which would destroy what
we have established as fundamental, concerning the
absolute reign of silence throughout the rest of the
piece, in favour of Virtue, the sole speaking party at
this instant, or third period of our history.

(4)   According to a computation, which in this
way of reasoning might be made, of the whole motion
or action to be given to our figure of Pleasure; she
should scarce have one-fifth reserved for that which
we may properly call active in her, and have already
termed her persuasive or indicative effort.   All besides
should be employed to express (if one may say so) her
inaction, her supineness, effeminacy, and indulgent ease.
The head and body might entirely favour this latter
passion.   One hand might be absolutely resigned to it;
serving only to support, with much ado, the lolling lazy
body.   And if the other hand be required to express
some kind of gesture or action toward the road of
pleasures recommended by this dame; the gesture
ought however to be slight and negligent, in the manner
of one who has given over speaking, and appears weary
and spent.

(5)   For the shape, the person, the complexion,
and what else may be further remarked as to the air
and manner of Pleasure; all this is naturally comprehended in the opposition, as above stated, between
herself and Virtue.

CHAPTER V

(1) It is sufficiently known, how great a liberty painters are used to take, in the colouring of their habits, and of other draperies belonging to their historical pieces. If they are to paint a Roman people, they represent them in different dresses; though it be certain the common people among them were habited very near alike, and much after the same colour. In like manner, the Egyptians, Jews, and other ancient nations, as we may well suppose, bore in this particular their respective likeness or resemblance one to another, as at present the Spaniards, Italians, and several other people of Europe. But such a resemblance as this would, in the way of painting, produce a very untoward effect; as may easily be conceived. For this reason the painter makes no scruple to introduce philosophers, and even apostles, in various colours, after a very extraordinary manner. It is here that the historical truth must of necessity indeed give way to that which we call poetical, as being governed not so much by reality, as by probability, or plausible appearance. So that a painter, who uses his privilege or prerogative in this respect, ought however to do it cautiously, and with discretion. And when occasion requires that he should present us his philosophers or apostles thus variously coloured, he must take care at least so to mortify his colours, that these plain poor men may not appear, in his piece, adorned like so many lords or princes of the modern garb.

R.   4

(2) If, on the other hand, the painter should happen to take for his subject some solemn entry or triumph, where, according to the truth of fact, all manner of magnificence had without doubt been actually displayed, and all sorts of bright and dazzling colours heaped together and advanced, in emulation, one against another; he ought on this occasion, in breach of the historical truth, or truth of fact, to do his utmost to diminish and reduce the excessive gaiety and splendour of those objects, which would otherwise raise such a confusion, oppugnancy, and riot of colours, as would to any judicious eye appear absolutely intolerable.

(3) It becomes therefore an able painter in this, as well as in the other parts of his workmanship, to have regard principally, and above all, to the agreement or correspondency of things. And to that end it is necessary he should form in his mind a certain note or character of unity, which being happily taken, would, out of the many colours of his piece, produce (if one may say so) a particular distinct species of an original kind: like those compositions in music, where among the different airs (such as sonatas, entries, or sarabands) there are different and distinct species; of which we may say in particular, as to each, "that it has its own proper character or genius, peculiar to itself."

(4) Thus the harmony of painting requires, "that in whatever key the painter begins his piece, he should be sure to finish it in the same."

(5) This regulation turns on the principal figure, or on the two or three which are eminent, in a tablature composed of many. For if the painter happens to give a certain height or richness of colouring to his principal figure; the rest must in proportion necessarily partake this genius. But if, on the contrary, the painter should have chanced to give a softer air, with more gentleness and simplicity of colouring, to his principal figure; the rest must bear a character proportionable, and appear

in an extraordinary simplicity; that one and the same
spirit may, without contest, reign through the whole of
his design.

(6)   Our historical draught of Hercules will afford
us a very clear example in the case. For considering
that the hero is to appear on this occasion retired and
gloomy; being withal in a manner naked, and without
any other covering than a lion's skin, which is itself
of a yellow and dusky colour; it would be really im-
practicable for a painter to represent this principal
figure in any extraordinary brightness or lustre. From
whence it follows, that in the other inferior figures
or subordinate parts of the work, the painter must
necessarily make use of such still quiet colours, as
may give to the whole piece a character of solemnity
and simplicity, agreeable with itself. Now should our
painter honestly go about to follow his historian, according to the literal sense of the history, which represents
Virtue to us in a resplendent robe of the purest and
most glossy white, it is evident he must after this
manner destroy his piece. The good painter in this,
as in all other occasions of like nature, must do as the
good poet; who undertaking to treat some common
and known subject, refuses however to follow strictly,
like a mere copyist or translator, any preceding poet
or historian; but so orders it, that his work in itself
becomes really new and original.

Publica materies privati juris erit, si
Nec circa vilem patulumque moraberis orbem;
Nec verbum verbo curabis reddere fidus
Interpres[1].

(7)   As for what relates to the perspective or scene
of our historical piece, it ought so to present itself, as
to make us instantly conceive that it is in the country,
and in a place of retirement, near some wood or forest,
that this whole action passes.   For it would be

---

[1] Horat. *de Art. Poet.* ll. 131-4.

impertinent to bring architecture or buildings of whatever kind in view, as tokens of company, diversion,
or affairs, in a place purposely chosen to denote
solitude, thoughtfulness, and premeditated retreat.
Besides, that according to the poets (our guides and
masters in this art) neither the goddesses, nor other
divine forms of whatever kind, cared ever to present
themselves to human sight, elsewhere than in these
deep recesses. And it is worth observing here, how
particularly our philosophical historian affects to speak,
by way of prevention, of the solitary place where
Hercules was retired, and of his thoughtfulness preceding this apparition: which from these circumstances
may be construed henceforward as a mere dream; but
as such, a truly rational, and divine one.

(8) As to the fortress, temple, or palace, of Virtue,
situated on a mountain, after the emblematical way,
as we see represented in some pieces formed upon this
subject; there is nothing of this kind expressed by our
historian. And should this or any thing of a like nature
present itself in our design, it would fill the mind with
foreign fancies, and mysterious views, no way agreeable to the taste and genius of this piece. Nor is there
any thing, at the same time, on Pleasure's side, to
answer, by way of opposition, to this palace of Virtue;
which, if expressed, would on this account destroy the
just simplicity and correspondency of our work.

(9) Another reason against the perspective part,
the architecture, or other studied ornaments of the
landscape kind, in this particular piece of ours, is, that
in reality there being no occasion for these appearances,
they would prove a mere incumbrance to the eye, and
would of necessity disturb the sight, by diverting it
from that which is principal, the history and fact.
Whatsoever appears in a historical design, which is
not essential to the action, serves only to confound
the representation, and perplex the mind: more particularly, if these episodic parts are so lively wrought,
as to vie with the principal subject, and contend for

precedency with the figures and human life. A just design, or tablature, should, at first view, discover, what nature it is designed to imitate; what life, whether of the higher or lower kind, it aims chiefly to represent. The piece must by no means be equivocal or dubious; but must with ease distinguish itself, either as historical and moral, or as perspective and merely natural. If it be the latter of these beauties, which we desire to see delineated according to its perfection, then the former must give place. The higher life must be allayed, and in a manner discountenanced and obscured; whilst the lower displays itself, and is exhibited as principal. Even that which according to a term of art we commonly call still-life, and is in reality of the last and lowest degree of painting, must have its superiority and just preference in a tablature of its own species. It is the same in animal pieces, where beasts or fowl are represented. In landscape, inanimates are principal: it is the earth, the water, the stones and rocks which live. All other life becomes subordinate. Humanity, sense, manners, must in this place yield, and become inferior. It would be a fault even to aim at the expression of any real beauty in this kind, or go about to animate or heighten in any considerable degree the accompanying figures of men, or deities which are accidentally introduced, as appendices, or ornaments, in such a piece. But if, on the contrary, the human species be that which first presents itself in a picture; if it be the intelligent life, which is set to view; it is the other species, the other life, which must then surrender and become subservient. The merely natural must pay homage to the historical or moral. Every beauty, every grace must be sacrificed to the real beauty of this first and highest order. For nothing can be more deformed than a confusion of many beauties: and the confusion becomes inevitable, where the subjection is not complete.

(10) By the word moral are understood, in this place, all sorts of judicious representations of the human

passions; as we see even in battle pieces; excepting those of distant figures, and the diminutive kind; which may rather be considered as a sort of landscape.   In all other martial pieces, we see expressed in lively action, the several degrees of valour, magnanimity, cowardice, terror, anger, according to the several characters of nations, and particular men.   It is here that we may see heroes and chiefs (such as the Alexanders or Constantines) appear, even in the hottest of the action, with a tranquillity and sedateness of mind peculiar to themselves: which is, indeed, in a direct and proper sense, profoundly moral.

(11)   But as the moral part is differently treated in a poem, from what it is in history, or in a philosophical work; so must it, of right, in painting be far differently treated, from what it naturally is, either in the history, or poem.   For want of a right understanding of this maxim, it often happens that by endeavouring to render a piece highly moral and learned, it becomes thoroughly ridiculous and impertinent.

(12)   For the ordinary works of sculpture, such as the low-relieves, and ornaments of columns and edifices, great allowance is made.   The very rules of perspective are here wholly reversed, as necessity requires, and are accommodated to the circumstance and genius of the place or building, according to a certain oeconomy or order of a particular and distinct kind; as will easily be observed by those who have thoroughly studied the Trajan and Antoninus pillars, and other relieve-works of the ancients.   In the same manner, as to pieces of engraved work, medals, or whatever shews itself in one substance (as brass or stone), or only by shade and light (as in ordinary drawings, or stamps), much also is allowed, and many things admitted, of the fantastic, miraculous, or hyperbolical kind.   It is here that we have free scope, withal, for whatever is learned, emblematical, or enigmatic.   But for the completely imitative and illusive art of painting, whose character

it is to employ in her works the united force of different
colours; and, who surpassing by so many degrees, and
in so many privileges, all other human fiction, or
imitative art, aspires in a directer manner towards
deceit, and a command over our very sense; she must of
necessity abandon whatever is over-learned, humorous,
or witty; to maintain herself in what is natural, credible,
and winning of our assent: that she may thus acquit
herself of what is her chief province, the specious
appearance of the object she represents. Otherwise
we shall naturally bring against her the just criticism
of Horace, on the scenical representation so nearly
allied to her:

Quodcunque ostendis mihi sic, incredulus odi.

(13) We are therefore to consider this as a sure
maxim or observation in painting, "that a historical
and moral piece must of necessity lose much of its
natural simplicity and grace, if any thing of the emblematical or enigmatic kind be visibly and directly intermixed." As if, for instance, the circle of the Zodiac[1],
with its twelve signs, were introduced. Now this being
an appearance which carries not any matter of similitude
or colourable resemblance to any thing extant in real
nature; it cannot possibly pretend to win the sense, or
gain belief, by the help of any poetical enthusiasm,
religious history, or faith. For by means of these,
indeed, we are easily induced to contemplate as realities
those divine personages and miraculous forms, which
the leading painters, ancient and modern, have speciously
designed, according to the particular doctrine or theo-
logy of their several religious and national beliefs. But
for our tablature in particular, it carries nothing with
it of the mere emblematical or enigmatic kind: since
for what relates to the double way of the vale and

---

[1] This is what Raphael himself has done, in his famous design of *The
Judgment of Paris*. But this piece having never been painted, but
designed only for Marc Antonio's engraving, it comes not within our
censure; as appears by what is said in the paragraph just preceding.

mountain, this may naturally and with colourable appearance be represented at the mountain's foot. But if on the summit or highest point of it, we should place the fortress, or palace of virtue, rising above the clouds, this would immediately give the enigmatical mysterious air to our picture, and of necessity destroy its persuasive simplicity, and natural appearance.

(14)   In short, we are to carry this remembrance still along with us, "that the fewer the objects are, besides those which are absolutely necessary in a piece, the easier it is for the eye, by one simple act and in one view, to comprehend the sum or whole." The multiplication of subjects, though subaltern, renders the subordination more difficult to execute in the ordinance or composition of a work. And if the subordination be not perfect, the order (which makes the beauty) remains imperfect. Now the subordination can never be perfect, except "when the ordinance is such, that the eye not only runs over with ease the several parts of the design (reducing still its view each moment on the principal subject on which all turns), but when the same eye, without the least detainment in any of the particular parts, and resting, as it were, immovable in the middle, or centre of the tablature, may see at once, in an agreeable and perfect correspondency, all which is there exhibited to the sight[1]."

---

[1] This is what the Grecian masters so happily expressed, by the single word εὐσύνοπτον.   See 'Characteristics' vol. I. pp. 143, etc.

CHAPTER VI

(1) THERE remains for us now to consider only of the separate ornaments, independent both of figures and perspective; such as the machine-work[1] or divinities in the sky, the winds, cupids, birds, animals, dogs, or other loose pieces which are introduced without any absolute necessity, and in a way of humour. But as these belong chiefly to the ordinary life, and to the comic or mixed kind; our tablature, which on the contrary is wholly epic, heroic, and in the tragic style, would not so easily admit of anything in this light way.

(2) We may besides consider, that whereas the mind is naturally led to fancy mystery in a work of such a genius or style of painting as ours, and to confound with each other the two distinct kinds of the emblematic and merely historical or poetic; we should take care not to afford it this occasion of error and deviation, by introducing into a piece of so uniform a design, such appendices, or supplementary parts, as, under pretext of giving light to the history, or characterizing the figures, should serve only to distract or dissipate the sight, and confound the judgment of the more intelligent spectators.

(3) "Will it then, says one, be possible to make out the story of these two dames in company with Hercules, without otherwise distinguishing them than as above described?"—We answer, it is possible; and

---

[1] This is understood of the machine-work, when it is merely ornamental, and not essential in the piece; by making part of the history, or fable itself.

not that only, but certain and infallible, in the case of
one who has the least genius, or has ever heard in
general concerning Hercules, without so much as
having ever heard this history in particular.   But if
notwithstanding this, we would needs add some exterior
marks, more declaratory and determinative of these
two personages, Virtue and Pleasure; it may be performed, however, without any necessary recourse to
what is absolutely of the emblem-kind.   The manner
of this may be explained as follows.

(4)   The energy or natural force of Virtue, according
to the moral philosophy of highest note among the
ancients, was expressed in the double effect of for-
bearance[1] and endurance, or what we may otherwise
call refrainment and support.   For the former, the bit
or bridle, placed somewhere on the side of Virtue, may
serve as emblem sufficient; and for the second, the
helmet may serve in the same manner; especially since
they are each of them appurtenances essential to heroes
(who, in the quality of warriors, were also subduers or
managers of horses[2]) and that at the same time these
are really portable instruments, such as the martial
dame; who represents virtue, may be well supposed
to have brought along with her.

(5)   On the side of Pleasure, certain vases, and
other pieces of embossed plate, wrought in the figures
of satyrs, fauns, and bacchanals, may serve to express
the debauches of the table-kind.   And certain draperies
thrown carelessly on the ground, and hung upon a neighbouring tree, forming a kind of bower and couch for
this luxurious dame, may serve sufficiently to suggest
the thought of other indulgences, and to support the
image of the effeminate, indolent, and amorous passions.
Besides that for this latter kind, we may rest satisfied,
it is what the painter will hardly fail of representing

---

[1] Καρτερία, Ἐγκράτεια : they were described as sisters in the emblematic moral philosophy of the ancients.   Whence that known precept,
Ἀνέχου καὶ Ἀπέχου, Sustine et Abstine.

[2] Castor, Pollux; all the heroes of Homer; Alexander the Great, etc.

to the full. The fear is, lest he should overdo this part, and express the affection too much to the life. The appearance will, no doubt, be strongly wrought in all the features and proportions of this third figure; which is of a relish far more popular, and vulgarly engaging, than that other opposed to it, in our historical design.

CONCLUSION

(1) WE may conclude this argument with a general reflection, which seems to arise naturally from what has been said on this subject in particular: "that in a real history-painter, the same knowledge, the same study, and views, are required, as in a real poet." Never can the poet (whilst he justly holds that name) become a relator, or historian at large. He is allowed only to describe a single action; not the actions of a single man, or people. The painter is a historian at the same rate, but still more narrowly confined, as in fact appears; since it would certainly prove a more ridiculous attempt to comprehend two or three distinct actions or parts of history in one picture, than to comprehend ten times the number in one and the same poem.

(2) It is well known, that to each species of poetry, there are natural proportions and limits assigned. And it would be a gross absurdity indeed to imagine, that in a poem there was nothing which we could call measure or number, except merely in the verse. An elegy, and an epigram have each of them their measure, and proportion, as well as a tragedy, or epic poem. In the same manner, as to painting, sculpture, or statuary, there are particular measures which form what we call a piece: as for instance, in mere portraiture, a head, or bust: the former of which must retain always the whole, or at least a certain part of the neck; as the latter the shoulders, and a certain part of the breast. If any thing be added or retrenched,

the piece is destroyed. It is then a mangled trunk, or dismembered body, which presents itself to our imagination; and this too not through use merely, or on the account of custom, but of necessity, and by the nature of the appearance: since there are such and such parts of the human body, which are naturally matched, and must appear in company: the section, if unskilfully made, being in reality horrid, and representing rather an amputation in surgery, than a seemly division or separation to art. And thus it is, that in general, through all the plastic arts, or works of imitation, "whatsoever is drawn from nature, with the intention of raising in us the imagination of natural species or object, according to real beauty and truth, should be comprised in certain complete portions, or districts, which represent the correspondency or union of each part of nature with entire nature herself." And it is this natural apprehension, or anticipating sense of unity, which makes us give even to the works of our inferior artisans, the name of pieces by way of excellence, and as denoting the justness and truth of work.

(3) In order therefore to succeed rightly in the formation of any thing truly beautiful in this higher order of design; it were to be wished that the artist, who had understanding enough to comprehend what a real piece or tablature imported, and who, in order to this, had acquired the knowledge of a whole and parts, would afterwards apply himself to the study of moral and poetic truth: that by this means the thoughts, sentiments, or manners, which hold the first rank in his historical work, might appear suitable to the higher and nobler species of humanity in which he practised, to the genius of the age which he described, and to the principal or main action which he chose to represent. He would then naturally learn to reject those false ornaments of affected graces, exaggerated passions, hyperbolical and prodigious forms; which equally with the mere capricious and grotesque, destroy the just simplicity and unity, essential in a piece. And for his

colouring; he would then soon find how much it became him to be reserved, severe, and chaste, in this particular of this art; where luxury and libertinism are, by the power of fashion and the modern taste, become so universally established.

(4) It is evident however from reason itself, as well as from history[1] and experience, that nothing is more fatal, either to painting, architecture, or the other arts, than this false relish, which is governed rather by what immediately strikes the sense, than by what consequentially and by reflection pleases the mind, and satisfies the thought and reason. So that whilst we look on painting with the same eye, as we view commonly the rich stuffs, and coloured silks worn by our ladies, and admired in dress, equipage, or furniture; we must of necessity be effeminate in our taste, and utterly set wrong as to all judgment and knowledge in the kind. For of this imitative art we may justly say; "that though it borrows help indeed from colours, and uses them, as means, to execute its designs; it has nothing, however, more wide of its real aim, or more remote from its intention, than to make a shew of colours, or from their mixture, to raise a separate[2] and flattering pleasure to the sense."

---

[1] See Vitruvius and Pliny.

[2] The pleasure is plainly foreign and *separate*, as having no concern or share in the proper delight or entertainment which naturally arises from the subject, and workmanship itself. For the subject, in respect of pleasure, as well as science, is absolutely completed, when the design is executed, and the proposed imitation once accomplished. And thus it always is the best, when the colours are most subdued, and made subservient.

TREATISE III
THE PICTURE OF CEBES
DISCIPLE OF
SOCRATES

TRANSLATED FROM THE GREEK
AND ACCOMPANIED WITH NOTES

ἀνέχειν καὶ ἀπέχειν

Printed in lieu of the unwritten 'Appendix concerning
the Emblem of Cebes'

THE PICTURE OF CEBES

DISCIPLE OF

SOCRATES[1]

TRANSLATED FROM THE GREEK[2]

WE were walking in the temple of Saturn, where we took a view of a great many other presents that were there. But there was placed before the temple a picture, in which there were certain drawings that were foreign and strange, and it contained certain particular fictions, that we were not able to guess what they were, nor whence they were taken. For the thing described seemed to us two neither a city nor a camp, but an enclosure that contained within it other enclosures, one greater, and one less. There was a gate in the first enclosure, and at the gate there seemed to stand a great crowd of people, and within the enclosure there appeared a multitude of women. At the entrance of the first gate and enclosure there stood an old man, who by his manner expressed his giving certain directions to the crowd that was entering[3]. When we had been long in doubt amongst ourselves, about the meaning and explication of these fictions, an elderly man accosting us said :

It is no wonder at all strangers, that you are at a loss about this picture; for there are not many of the

---

[1] [Cf. Prefatory Introduction, *supra*, p. xviii.]

[2] From Κέβητος Πίναξ.

[3] It is the entrance into the moral life, and not the natural that is here described. Of consequence the crowd here are of years to begin their rational faculties and to have a sense of their own in moral concerns.

country that understand what the fiction imparts. For it is not a present made by any citizen, but a long time ago, there came hither a certain stranger, a man of great prudence and wisdom, one who both in his words and action pursued that method of life, that was followed by Pythagoras and Parmenides[1], and this man erected this temple and dedicated this picture to Saturn.

Did you know this man then, said I, and have you seen him?

Yes, said he, and long admired him, for when I was a young man I have heard him discourse upon many noble subjects, and have often heard him explain the meaning of this fiction.

Pray then, said I, unless you have some urgent business on your hands relate it to us for we are mighty desirous to hear what this fiction means.

Strangers said he, I do not at all grudge you that satisfaction, but this you must understand, that the relation carries something of danger with it.

And what is that? said I.

Why, said he, that if you give attention and understand the things that are told you, you will become wise and happy; but if you do not you will become fools and unhappy, vicious and ignorant, and will pass your days wretchedly. For this relation is like the riddle that the sphinx used to propose to men. If a man understood it he came off with safety, but if he understood it not he was destroyed by the sphinx. It is the same with this relation, for folly is a sphinx in men. She makes dark representations to man of what is good, and of what is ill, and of what is neither good nor ill in life. And if a man do not attain to the knowledge of these things he perishes under her hands, and not all at once, as he who dies devoured by the sphinx, but he wastes away and perishes little by little during the whole course of his life, like those that are

---

[1] See Note (2) *infra*, p. 87.

delivered over to torture.   But if a man attain to this knowledge then folly on the other hand perishes, the man is saved, and he becomes blessed and happy in the whole course of his life.   Do you therefore give attention, and do not lend an idle ear.

O Hercules, if this be the case what a vast desire have you inspired us with.

Indeed, said he, this is the case.

Haste then and give us the relation as being men that will give attention, and that not slightly, since the consequences both ways are of great importance. Taking a wand therefore into his hand, and holding it up to the picture,

You see, said he, this enclosure.

We see it.

This in the first place you must know that this is called life, and that mighty crowd that stands at the gate, these are they that are upon their entrance into life.   The old man that stands above holding a paper in one hand, and seems to be showing something with the other, is called the divine genius.   He directs those that are going in, what they ought to do when they are entered into life, and shows them the way they ought to take, if they would obtain safety in life.

And what is the way therefore, said I, that he leads them to take, or how are they to proceed ?

You see near the gate, said he, a seat that stands at that place where the crowd enters ; and upon it sits a woman whose form is artfully composed, and her appearance engaging, holding a kind of cup in her hand.

I see her, said I, but who is she?

She is called deceit, said he, and leads all men astray.

And what is it that she does ?

She gives a draught of her own power and nature to those that are entering into life.

And what is this draught ?

Error, said he, and ignorance.

What follows upon this ?

When they have taken this draught, they enter into life.

Do all drink of error, or do they not ?

All drink of it, said he, but some more and some less.—Now don't you see besides within the gate a multitude of courtesans of all kinds of shapes and figures ?

I do.

These are called opinions, desires, and pleasures, and when the crowd enters these run to them, and severally engage themselves to every one, and lead them away.

And whither do they lead them ?

Some to safety, and others to destruction, by means of deceit.

O unfortunate man, how sad a draught is this that you speak of!

And yet they all give assurance that they will conduct them to what is blest and to a life that is happy and advantageous. Some by means of ignorance and error that they drank from the cup of deceit, do not find the true way in life, but wander about at random as you see. And you see how they that first entered rove about wherever these courtesans direct them.

I see it, said I, but what is that woman that seems to be a blind distracted creature, and stands upon a round stone ?

She is called fortune, said he, and she is not only blind but distracted and deaf.

And what is her business ?

Why she rambles about everywhere, said he, some she robs of what they possess and gives it to others, then she immediately takes from these very persons the things that she gave them, and gives them to others again, immediately and as chance directs, so that her ensign very well explains her nature.

What is the ensign, said I ?

Her standing upon a round stone.

And what does this import ?

Why that her gifts are neither secure nor stable. For the losses and disappointments are very great and very severe, when anyone reposes any trust in her.

And that mighty crowd that stands about her, what would they have and what are they called ?

These are called the inconsiderate, and all beg for the things that she throws about.

And how comes it to pass then that they do not all carry countenances alike, but that some seem to rejoice, and others are in dejection and have their arms extended ?

Those of them that seem to rejoice and laugh are such as have received something at the hands of fortune, and these call her good fortune, they that seem to be in tears and have their arms extended, are those from whom she has taken the things she had before given them, and these on the other hand call her ill fortune.

But what are the things she gives them that the receivers are so rejoiced at, and they that part with them lament for with tears ?

These, said he, are such things as by the multitude are accounted good.

But what are they ?

They are smiles, honour, noble birth, children, tyrannies, kingships, and other things like these.

And how comes it to pass then that these things are not good ?

Concerning these matters, said he, we will discourse at another time.   But now let us mind the explication of the fiction.

Be it so.

You see therefore, when you have passed this gate, another enclosure that stands higher, and certain women that stand without the enclosure, and are adorned as courtesans used to be.

Yes, I do.

These are called intemperance, prodigality, insatiableness, and flattery.

And why do they stand there?

They keep a watch upon those that have received anything from fortune.

And what then?

They run to them and engage themselves with them, and flatter them, and tell them that they shall enjoy a life of pleasure, without trouble, and without misfortune. If anyone therefore happens to be persuaded by them into luxury, then as far as certain bounds go, his commerce with her appears agreeable and pleasant, while she tickles the man, but afterwards it continues so no longer; for when he recovers his senses he perceives that it is not he that has fed, but that he has been fed upon and abused by her. And when she has wasted all that he has received from fortune, he is forced to be a slave to these women, to suffer everything, to act a vile indecent part, and for their sake to do everything that is pernicious; such as to defraud, to plunder places that are sacred, to swear falsely, to betray, to rob, and all things that are of the like kind. Then when everything fails them, they are delivered over to torture.

And what is she?

A little behind these women you see, said he, a kind of little door and a place that's narrow and dark?

I do.

And certain vile filthy women clothed in rags seem to be there assembled?

It is so.

Of these therefore, said he, she that holds a scourge is called torture; she that holds her head between her knees is called grief; she that is tearing her hair vexation.

But he that stands by these women is of ugly aspect, lank in shape and naked, and she that is also like him, lank and ugly, who are they?

He, said he, is called anguish, and she his sister despair. To these therefore is the man delivered; with these he passes his days in torment; then again he is thrown into another apartment to misery; and thus he passes the remainder of his life in all kind of misery, unless by fortune's means repentance meet with him.

Then what happens, if repentance meets with him?

She takes him out of these evils and gives him another opinion, and another desire that conducts him towards true learning, but likewise towards her, who is called false learning.

And what happens upon this?

If he admits, said he, of that opinion that conducts him towards true learning, he is by her purified and saved and becomes blessed and happy in the whole course of his life. If he does not admit of her, he is again led astray by false opinion.

O Hercules how great is this other danger! But what is false learning? said I.

Do not you see that other enclosure?

I do, said I.

And without the enclosure does not there stand a woman, who appears extremely clean and decent?

There does.

This woman the generality of man and the inconsiderate call learning, yet she is not so but she is the false learning, said he, and they who at last obtain safety when they have a mind to proceed to true learning first touch here.

Is there not another way therefore that leads to true learning?

There is, said he.

But those men who walk to and fro, within the enclosure, who are they?

These are the lovers of false learning, but are deceived and think that they are conversing with true learning.

And what are these called?

These are some of their poets, said he, some skilled in rhetoric, some in the art of discoursing, some in music, some in arithmetic, some in geometry, some in astronomy, some are patrons of pleasure, some Peripatetics[1], some critics, and people of the like kind.

But those women that seem to be running about, and that resemble those others among whom you said that intemperance and her attendants were, who are they?

These are the very same persons, said he.

And have they therefore entrance here?

Yes indeed they have but it is but sparingly, and not as within the first enclosure.

And have opinions too access hither?

They have, said he, for the draught these men took from the cup of deceit, ignorance, too, and together with her, even folly, remains still with them. Nor does opinion quit them, nor the rest of the vicious train, till renouncing false learning they enter into the true way, and take a draught that has the power of cleansing them from the taint of the former, till they throw off all the vices they retain, till they throw off opinion, ignorance, and every other vice; and thus they will be saved. But while they continue with false learning they will never be set free; nor will they get rid of any vice by means of these sciences.

Which is the way then that leads to true learning?

Do you see that place above where nobody inhabits, but that seems deserted?

I see it.

You see then a certain little gate, and a way that leads to that gate that is not much crowded and where very few are passing, it appears to be very rough and rocky, and passable with great difficulty.

I do, said I.

Then there appears to be a high hill, whose ascent is extremely narrow with deep precipices on both sides of it.

I see it.

This therefore, said he, is the way that leads to true learning.

[1] See Note (3), *infra*, p. 87.

Truly 'tis trouble even to look at.

Then don't you see above, round the hill, a rock that is of great extent, high and a precipice all round? I see it, said I.

You see then two women standing upon this rock, who are in good plight, robust and healthy, and hold out their hands with great earnestness.

I see them, but what are they called? said I.

The one is called abstinence, and the other patience, and they are sisters.

And why do they hold out their hands with such earnestness?

They exhort those that approach the place, said he, to take courage and not to sink under their difficulties, telling them they ought to bear up yet a little while, and that then they will get into a very fair and beautiful way.

And when they get up to the rock how do they mount it? For I see no way that leads up to it.

These women descend from the rocks toward them, and draw them up to themselves. Then they bid them rest themselves, and after a little time they give them strength and courage, they promise to place them with true learning, and they show them the way, how fair it is, how smooth, how easily passable, and how clean and free from all defects, as you see.

Indeed it appears so.

And then do you see above that grove a certain place that appears to be very beautiful, is like a meadow, and has a great deal of light upon it?

I do.

And do you observe in the middle of that meadow another enclosure, and another gate?

It is so. But what is this place called?

The habitation of the happy, said he, for here dwell all the virtues and happiness herself.

I allow, said I, that it is indeed a very beautiful place.

You see then, said he, that by the gate there is

a beautiful woman, her countenance sedate, having already attained to the middle and most judicious part of her age, in a plain dress, and without any affected ornaments, and she stands not upon a round stone, but upon a square one, that rests upon the ground with great firmness, and that with her there are two others that seem to be her daughters.

It appears so.

Of these she that is in the middle is called learning ; one is called truth, and the other persuasion.

And why does she stand upon a square stone ?

It is her ensign, said he, and imports that the way to her is firm and secure to those that receive them.

And what are the things she gives ?

Courage and intrepidity, said he.

And what are these ?

They consist in knowing how never to suffer anything severe or ill in life.

O Hercules, said I, what noble gifts ! But for what reason does she stand so without the enclosure ?

That she may attend the cure of those that come up to her, and give them a draught of her own cleansing nature. When they are cleansed, she introduces them to the virtues.

How is this, said I, for I do not understand it ?

But, said he, you will understand, that if a man happens to be extremely sick, and applying himself to a physician, shall discharge all the causes of his distemper by purging medicines, the physician then presents him to recovery and health. But that if he do not submit to the things the physician ordered him, he is then justly rejected and perishes under his distemper.

This I understand, said I.

In the same manner therefore, when anyone comes to learning, she takes care of his cure and gives him a draught of her own nature and power, that she may first cleanse away and discharge all the ills he came with.

And what are these ?

Ignorance and error that he drank from the cup of deceit ; arrogance, desire, intemperance, wrath, love of money, and all those things that he was filled with in the first enclosure.

When he is cleansed therefore, whither does she send him ?

She sends him in, said he, to knowledge, and to the other virtues.

And what are these ?

Do not you see, said he, without the gate, a set of women, how handsome they appear to be, and how decent in plain habits, no way effeminate and nice ? And besides how artless they are, and without any of these affected ornaments that the others have ?

I see them, said I.   But what are they called ?

The first of them, said he, is called knowledge ; and the others are her sisters, fortitude, justice, integrity, modesty, decency, freedom, abstinence and gentleness.

O the beautiful personages ! said I, how great are the hopes we have ?

Yes, said he, if you understand the things that you hear, and make them habitual to you.

We will use our utmost care in it, said I.

Then, said he, you will be saved.

But then when these women have received him, whither do they conduct him ?

To their mother, said he.

Who is she ?

Happiness, said he.

And what is she ?

You see a road that leads to that building that stands aloft, and is the summit of all the enclosure ?

I see it.

And at the porch there sits a sedate comely woman, upon a lofty seat, in a liberal but plain and unaffected dress, and crowned with a flourishing crown, in a very beautiful manner.

So it appears to be.

This therefore is happiness, said he.

When therefore anyone gets thither, what does he do?

Happiness crowns him with her own nature and power, and so do all the other virtues, as those are crowned who have gained a victory in the greatest conflicts.

And what are these conflicts he has conquered in? said I.

In the greatest, said he, and he has subdued wild beasts of the greatest size; and such as before devoured, tortured and enslaved him. All these he has conquered and thrown from him, and he is become master of himself, so as that they are now slaves to him as he was before to them.

And what are these beasts you speak of? for I am very desirous to be informed of it.

In the first place, said he, ignorance and error, and do you not take these to be beasts?

Yes, said I, and very mischievous ones.

Then grief, anguish, love of money, intemperance, and the rest of the vicious train, all these he has subdued, and is no longer subdued by them as before.

O the noble acts, said I, and the noble victory! But pray tell me this too, what is the power of that crown, that you said he was crowned with?

A power, young man, that makes him happy. For he that is crowned with this power becomes blessed and happy, and places his hopes of happiness no longer in other things but himself.

O how noble a conquest is that you speak of! But when he is crowned, what does he do or whither does he go?

The virtues take him and conduct him to that place, from whence he came before; and show him the people that pass their time there, how ill and how wretched they live, how they make shipwreck in life, wander and are led about in subjection, as if subdued by enemies, some by intemperance, some by arrogance, some by love of money, some by vanity, and others by other vices. And of these evils, that they are hampered with, they are not able to extricate themselves, so as to be saved and to reach this place, but they pass their days in hurry and disorder; and this they undergo because they are not able to find their way to this place, for they have forgot the commands of the divinity.

I think you say very right, but then this again, I am at a loss about, why the virtues should show him the place from whence he came before.

He was not exactly apprized, nor did he understand, said he, any of the things that passed there; but was at a loss, and by reason of ignorance and error, that he had sucked in, he took things that were not good to be good, and things that were not ill to be ill; by which means he lived wretchedly as others do who inhabit there. But now having attained to the knowledge of things profitable and advantageous, he lives handsomely and views how wretchedly those others fare.

When therefore he has viewed all these things, what does he do and whither does he go?

Wherever he pleases, said he, for he has security everywhere, as much as if he were possessed of the Corycian cavern[1]. And wherever he comes he will take every step in life handsomely and well, and with all manner of security. For all men will receive him joyfully, as patients do their physician.

And is he not at all afraid of suffering at the hands of those women that you called beasts?

Not at all, for he is not to be disordered, either by vexation or grief, or intemperance, or love of money, or fear of poverty, or by any other ill; for he is master

---

[1] In the ascent of the mountain Parnassus, from Delphi, there is a cavern called Corycian from a nymph Corygia. It is said to have been sacred to the nymphs and to Pan. The ascent to it from Delphi is passable for a mule or horse; but from the cavern to the summit of the mountain the ascent is difficult even for a man.

of them all, and is above all these things that afflicted him before, like those that deal in vipers. For these animals that do all others mischief, even to death, give them no pain because they have an antidote; so nothing affects this man because he has an antidote.

I think you say right, but tell me this further; who are those that seem to be coming from thence down the hill, some of them crowned and giving signs of satisfaction, some without crowns in an abject condition, who seem to have their legs and their heads bruised, and are held by a certain woman?

They that are crowned are such as have safely attained to learning, and are in joy upon their having gained her. They that are without crowns are such as have been rejected by learning, and are returning back in a vile and wretched condition; and such as losing all courage, after having mounted as far as patience, do again turn back and rave about without pursuing any certain way.

But those women that attend them, who are they?

Grief, said he, and vexations, despair, ignominy and ignorance.

All manner of evils you then say attend them.

All manner of evils, said he, do indeed attend them, and when they come into the first enclosure to luxury and intemperance, they do not blame themselves, but they presently fall to defame learning. And they tell how calamitous, wretched, and unhappy, they are who direct their course thither, who quitting that method of life, which they themselves pursue, pass their days in misery, and do not enjoy the good and valuable things that they themselves are possessed of.

What are the things that they call good?

Dissolution and intemperance, as one may in short express it. For to be cramming themselves like beasts they take to be the enjoyment of the greatest good in the world.

But those other women, that are coming from

thence, who are cheerful and laughing, what are they called?

Opinions, said he, who having conducted to learning, those, that are introduced to the virtues, turn back again in order to fetch more. And they relate how happy those already are, that they before conducted.

And have these then, said I, entrance to the virtues?

No, said he, for it is not allowed that opinions should have entrance to knowledge. But opinions deliver men to learning, and when learning has received them, they then turn back again, and freight anew with other effects.

These things I think you have related very well; but you have not yet discovered to us what it is that divinity directs those to do that are entering into life.

He bids them to courage, said he. And do you therefore take courage for I will relate all to you and not omit anything.

You speak very kindly and handsomely, said I.

Therefore holding out his hand again, you see, said he, that woman, that seems to be blind, and to stand upon a round stone, and that I lately told you was called fortune.

We see her.

He bids them put no trust in her, and not to believe that they have firm and secure possession of anything whatever, that any of them receive from her, not to account it their own; for nothing hinders her from taking those things away and giving them to others. For this she is frequently accustomed to do; and for this reason, he bids them not to subject themselves to her for the presents that she makes them, and neither to rejoice when she gives, nor to be dejected when she takes away; and neither to reproach her nor commend her. For she does nothing with reason, but at random, and as things fall out, as I told you before. For this reason therefore the divinity orders, that men should wonder at nothing that she does, and they should not resemble corrupt bankers, for these people when they receive money from men, are delighted and reckon it their own, but when they are called upon to return it they take offence, and think that they suffer great hardship, not remembering that they received these deposits to this very end, that the person depositing them may take them away again without any hinderance. The divinity therefore orders that men should be just so disposed with respect to the presents of fortune, and should remember that she is of such a nature, as to take away the things she has given, and again immediately to bestow abundance more, then presently to take away the things she so gives, and not only those, but what men were possessed of before. He orders therefore that they should receive the things that she gives, and with them go their way quietly to obtain a stable and secure gift.

And what is this? said I.

The gift that they will receive from learning, if they safely attain to her.

And what is that?

The true knowledge, said he, of things profitable, and this is a secure gift, stable and unchangeable. Therefore he orders men to fly quickly to her, and when they are come to these women that I said were called intemperance and luxury, he bids them quickly depart thence and to trust to none of those neither in anything till they come to false learning, and here he bids them pass sometimes, take what they think fit from her, as provision upon their journey, and then quickly to pass on to true learning. These are the things that the divinity enjoins. Whoever therefore acts contrary to these in anything, or gives but slight attention to them, is a wretch and perishes wretchedly. And now strangers, the fiction that is contained in the picture is such as I have related. But if you would make any further inquiry concerning any of the particulars, I grudge you not the satisfaction of knowing for I will tell it you.

What you say, said I, is very kind and handsome.
What is it then that the divinity bids them take from
false learning?

The things that seem to be of use.

And what are these?

Letters, said he, and some part of other sciences,
that like a kind of bridle as Plato says[1], have a power
to hinder young men from being drawn away to other
things.

And is it necessary for anyone that is to attain to
the true learning to take these things or not?

There is no necessity for it, said he. They are
of use, indeed, but they contribute nothing of themselves to the constituting men better.

Do you say that these things are of no use to the
making men better?

Men may become better without them, yet they
are not without their uses[2]. For as we sometimes
understand what is said by an interpreter, yet it is not
a useless thing for us to gain a more exact knowledge,
though we made shift to understand something of it
before. So that nothing hinders but that we may be
very well without these sciences.

And have these men of science no advantage
above the rest of men with respect to their being
better?

How can they have any such advantage when they
appear to be deceived both with respect to things that
are good and things that are ill, and are still hampered
by vices of all kinds? For there is no inconsistency
for a man to have skill in letters and to be master of
all the sciences, and yet at the same time to be a
drunkard, to be intemperate, to love money, to be
unjust, treacherous and to conclude to be a fool.

Indeed there are many such to be seen.

Wherefore, how can these men, said he, have the

---

[1] The Laws, Bk. VII, 808.
[2] There seems to be some defect that has occasioned the sense to be
not perfectly clear.

advantage with respect to their being better than others upon the account of these sciences?

From this discourse it does not appear by any means that they can. But what is the reason, said I, that they pass their time within the second enclosure as if they were neighbours to true learning?

What advantage is this to them, said he, when it is frequently to be seen, that there are those who come out of the first enclosure, from intemperance and the rest of the vicious train, even up to the third enclosure, to true learning, and yet quit these men of science? So that still how have these men the advantage? They are then less industrious, or have a sort of science that makes them worse than others.

How so? said I.

Because being within the second enclosure, if there be nothing else in the case, they fancy that they know things, that they really do not know; and while they are possessed with this opinion they must of necessity be less industrious with respect to any inclination to attain true learning. But then do not you see another thing, that opinions from out of the first enclosure have entrance to them here likewise? So that these men are not at all better than the others, unless repentance meet with them, and they become convinced that they are not possessed of learning but of the false learning that leads them astray, and that while they are in this disposition they can never be saved. Do you therefore strangers, said he, act in this manner. Dwell upon the things that have been told you, till you have made them habitual. You must frequently consider them and not give them over, and must reckon all other things but slight and occasional. If you do otherwise you will reap no benefit by the things you hear.

We will do it. But then relate to us how it comes to pass, that those things are not good, that men receive from fortune, such as life, health, riches and honour, children, conquests, and things of the like kind, and on the other hand how the contraries to these come not to be ill. For the assertion seems to us to be very strange and incredible.

Well then, said he, do you do your endeavour, in reply to me, to tell me how matters appear in such things as I shall ask you.

I will do it, said I.

If anyone then live wretched and ill, is life a good to him?

I think it is said but an ill.

How comes living then to be a good since to him it is an ill.

Because, to those that live wretchedly and ill, life I think is an ill, but to those that live handsomely and well, I think it is a good.

You say then that life is both good and ill.

I do.

Do not talk absurdly, for it is impossible that the same thing should be both good and ill. For by this means it would be both advantageous and hurtful at the same time.

Of a truth this is absurd. But how comes it to pass that, if living ill be an ill, to him that it may happen to, that life itself should be an ill?

For to live and live ill, said he, is not the same thing. Does it not appear so to you?

Truly it does not appear to me to be the same thing.

Therefore to live is not an ill; since if it were an ill, it would be an ill to those that live well, because they have life which is an ill.

I think you say true.

Therefore since living belongs both to those that live ill, and to those that live well, to live is neither good nor ill. So[1] cutting and burning in the case of distempered people, are not both noxious and salutary. Thus do matters stand with respect to life. Consider

---

[1] Here as well as in other pieces in the course for this reasoning there seem to be defects that have lost us the full strength of it.

then this. Would you choose to live wretchedly and ill, or to die handsomely and bravely?

I would choose to die handsomely.

Then neither is death an ill, since it is frequently more eligible than life.

These things are as you say.

The reason is the same with respect to health and sickness, for health frequently may not be of advantage, but the contrary when circumstances so fall out.

You say true.

Well then, let us examine in the same manner concerning riches, may we not take it for granted as a thing frequently to be seen, that riches are in a man's possession and yet that the man passes his days in wretchedness and misery?

Yes indeed one may see many such.

Riches then do not give any help to these men towards living handsomely and well.

It does not appear that they do, for they are vile unworthy men.

Therefore it is not riches that makes men deserving, but learning.

Probably it is so from this reasoning.

Then how can riches be a good if they do not help those that have them to be better men?

It appears to be as you say.

So neither is it of advantage or profit for some people to be rich, when they know not how to make use of riches.

So I think.

Therefore how can one judge that to be a good, that is often of no profit or advantage to have?

One cannot do it by any means.

Therefore if a man know how to make a skilful and handsome use of riches, he will live well, if not he will live ill.

I think you say very true in this.

And on the whole to pay a veneration to those things as being good, or to hold them in disgrace, as being ill, this is the thing that disorders men and does them mischief, while they put a mighty value on these things, and think to obtain happiness by means of them alone. They of consequence put all in practice in order to obtain them, even things that appear to be most impious. And all this they suffer by ignorance of good.

Notes[1] on the Picture of Cebes

(1) Diogenes Laertius in his preface ascribes the rise of philosophy to the Greeks, but he mentions several others to give it to the barbarians. This difference seems to be a matter that can never be composed. For where a rich and regular language was once formed, and the complete use of letters attained to, in that place the foundation of all science laid; but language and letters can hardly be supposed to be perfected but in a course of many ages. And letters can record nothing till they are perfected.

The birth, the infancy, and growth of letters therefore can never be known. But this much may be said in this matter, that it is letters, arts sciences, philosophy, that must establish the distinction between Greek and Barbarian. And a time there was before letters had their birth. Before that time then, all the several herds of men were equally barbarian, and if this infant production arose amongst the Greeks it still arose in a notion that was barbarian. And perhaps many nations may have nursed up this infant to a certain degree, but by means of distemper in government and by tyranny they have dropped it, and still kept in barbarism. It does not seem impossible, but that Egypt may have been the birthplace of Greek letters. From Egypt these people may have united themselves in Crete and in the isles of the Aegean sea, and may have settled colonies upon the continent in many

---

[1] [Cf. Prefatory Introduction, *supra*, p. xviii.]

places, and upon disorders in their mother-country and upon the erecting some mighty tyranny there these colonies may have preserved independency, liberty and letters. The Greeks in their several, free and independent states certainly nursed up learning to a prodigious perfection, and to the Greeks is the present world indebted for what they have of it.

The turn that was given to learning amongst the Gymnosophists, Druides, Chaldaeans and Mages, that were the wise men of the Indians, Gauls, Assyrians, and Persians, and the turn given to it by the Egyptians, as Laertius and others have described it, seem to imply that it was wrapped up in a mystery amongst them, kept within a few hands and communicated in ways not very intelligible, the professors of it more highly interested in the state and used their learning to serve political ends and to manage the multitude to their own purposes. And these are rather arguments of their imposture that was pretty apparent than of their learning that they in a great measure concealed. The antiquity of the Mages is reported to have been very great. Zoroaster, the first of them, is by some placed six thousand years before the taking of Troy, which exceeds the time that we set for the creation of the world. And Ephesus or Vulcan the son of Nile, to whom the Egyptians ascribe the original of learning, is reported by them to have lived forty-eight thousand eight hundred and sixty years before the time of Alexander the Great. Laertius mentions Musaeus, the son of Eumolpus, of the Athenian race; and Linus, the son of Hermes, or Mercury, and of the Muse Ouranie, a Theban, as men from whom learning is derived, but he is not particular as to the age they lived in.

The birth of the word Philosophy may perhaps be justly enough limited to the age of Thales and Pythagoras. For what before was called *sophia* or wisdom Pythagoras termed philosophy or love of wisdom ; and its followers, instead of wise men and sophists that they were called before, he named philosophers or lovers of wisdom, declaring that no man was wise, but that God only was so. But then one must have a very wrong notion of learning to think that it did not require a vast extent of time to arrive at the great perfection it had attained in that age and long before.

Can one believe that the poems of Homer were the product of letters in their infancy? Or can one imagine that the Spartan institution of Lycurgus was the product of an age when the first rudiments of letters and science were just appearing? Yet some place the birth of Homer an hundred and twelve years after the taking of Troy, and this is reckoned about four hundred and thirty years before the birth of Thales. Others make Homer contemporaneous with Lycurgus, who gave laws to Sparta about two hundred and fifty-eight years after the taking of Troy, which is about two hundred and eighty-six years before the birth of Thales. And Thales' birth preceded that of Socrates by about 170 years, and that of our Saviour Christ by about 637 years.

Laertius makes mention of schools of philosophy. One he calls the Ionic from Thales who was an Ionian, the other he calls Italic from Pythagoras, who passed most of his time in Italy. He divides philosophy into three parts: the natural from enquiring into the nature of the world, and things in it; the moral from the study of life and manners and of things that relate to ourselves; the dialectic from the study of the art of reasoning. And Socrates introduces the moral. And this may be truly said of Socrates, if no more be understood by it, than that he censured the vain philosophy of the naturalists, and endeavoured to turn men more to the study and knowledge of themselves. But that Socrates was the first father of the moral science seems to be an idle imagination. Diogenes Laertius then ranks the philosophers under several names, and mentions ten sorts of moral philosophy.

But notwithstanding that variety one may divide the
moral philosophy into three sorts ; one that establishes
a Providence disposing all things in the most beautiful
order, and giving to man a capacity to attend to its
laws and to follow them ; another that attributes the
disposition of things to atoms and chance and that
makes the pursuit of pleasure its end ; and the third
that takes part neither way, but judges things not to
be at all comprehensible, and therefore suspends opinion
entirely. Socrates and the branch derived from Chry-
sippus were of the first sort, Aristippus and Epicurus
of the second, and Pyrrho of the third. Other sects
seem necessarily to fall within compass of these three,
and to consist of various mixtures of them. The
picture writ by Cebes and the manual of Epictetus
are two little pieces that apparently belong to the
divine system of philosophy, and Cebes was one of
those who knew and conversed with Socrates.

(2) Parmenides was of the school of Pythagoras.
The succession in this school was thus Pherecydes,
Pythagoras, his son Telauges, Xenophanes, Parmen-
ides, Zeno the Eleatic, Leucippus, Democritus, who is
said to have been one year older than Socrates,
Nausiphanes, and Naucydes ; and from the two last,
Epicurus, Diog. Laertius, Proceus, Segment.

(3) The mention of the Peripatetics here and of
Plato afterward is used as an argument that Cebes
who conversed with Socrates was never the author of
this piece. But supposing that the name of Peripatetic
was not applied to any sort of men before Aristotle,
yet Cebes may very well have lived beyond the time
that this name was given to Aristotle and his followers.
For Aristotle was thirty-five years of age when Plato
died, and Cebes may have lived yet longer than Plato,
though Plato is reckoned to have been but 28 years
of age when Socrates died, and lived 80 years.

TREATISE IV

PLASTICS

OR

THE ORIGINAL PROGRESS

AND

POWER OF DESIGNATORY ART

ὅ τι καλὸν φίλον ἀεί.
Eurip. *Bacch.* 881.

Written in Italy in the year M.DCC.XII ; and edited
in the year M.DCCCC.XII.

PLASTICS

AN EPISTOLARY EXCURSION

IN

THE ORIGINAL PROGRESS

AND

POWER OF DESIGNATORY ART

1. CHARACTERS[1], 1st, 2d, 3d.

Distinction of characters, viz. first; second; third: viz. middle or mixed.

(1) FIRST. *Notes.* Marks of sounds, syllables, words, speech, and of sentiments, senses, meanings by that medium, viz. of sounds and speech. Thus ciphers, shorthand, Cicero's invention.

(2) SECOND. *Signs. Signa. Sigilla.* Imitation of real forms and natural beings, plastically (convex or concave), or lineally and graphically by lines and colours, from the superficies and extremities of the bodies, according to optics.

(3) A THIRD and middle sort, emblematic. As when the latter signa are used as mediums (speech being passed over) to convey sentiments, senses, meanings, etc. (but not sentences, diction, etc.) For when the figure of an animal stands as a mark,

---

[1] In the notes below for memory sake and order (all being smooth and polite above) place this table:

Characters

First — Alphabetical, verbal, shorthand, ciphers, numerical or arithmetical, mathematical, algebraical.

Second

Plastical
1. Embossing, or relief-work. / Statuary.
2. Stucco-work, outcut lapidary work. / Convex-works.
3. Engraving, etching, seal-work. / Concave or hollow-work.

Graphical

1. Clavo serrano or two colours
   1. Regular and natural according to just perspective.
   2. Irregular and without or by a contrary rule of perspective: as I. anaglyphics, 2. grotesque.
      1. Anaglyphical or lapidary according to the ancient relief-works, columns, friezes and sculptures emblematical and historical, such in particular as the works of Polidore da Carravaggio, disciple of Raphael.
      2. Arabesque, grotesque work, chimerical and capricious forms, border works, flourishes, etc. All which in two colours, at least not full coloured. For if so false, for reason given in Notion, chap. V, par. 12.

Middle or Third

1. True, natural and simple
   - Full coloured and perfect: Such as anciently Apelles and Protagoras. And among moderns, Raphael, the first raisers and perfectioners of art.
   - Emblematical* designs: whether graphical or plastic. The Greek and Roman anaglyphics of this narrative, historical or didactic, with what answers to the same in drawings, prints, etc. Paintings or full colours have hardly place here: because of wrong situation, loss of distances, and confusion of perspective.
2. False, barbarous and mixed
   - Enigmatical*, preposterous, disproportionable, gouty and lame forms. False imitation, lie, impotence, pretending. Egyptian hieroglyphics. Magical, mystical, monkish and Gothic emblems.

---

* I make no scruple to place the emblematic and enigmatic kind (which is a middle sort, holding something of each) as the third or last n order, even in respect of time, history, and progress of the arts. Since hardly will anyone imagine by reason and experience of all other nations, barbarians and Gothic as well as Greek, but that letters next follow upon speech, and the copy of forms afterward as a work of leisure. This second way of description or characters may indeed whilst yet rude

arbitrarily and without relation to his form, nature, passion, history, then is this no more than an ordinary first character (as α, β, γ).   But if natural history, passion, habit, form, be taken in, then ought this to be fine and beautiful and just: else it is lame and imperfect in its kind.

Of this latter sort, the *true*, therefore, is emblematic and graceful without mixture; the *false* enigmatic merely, mixt and barbarous: as the Egyptian hieroglyphics[1].   Nor can the mixture of middle characters with first, as in the Egyptian way of obelisks, be any other than monstrous upon examination, as it appears *prima facie* to the slightest examiner or novice: however this hieroglyphic may have been extolled by travelling philosophers and admirers of the wonders of Egypt.

That our particular science therefore, of design or signature may emerge from this chaos of barbarity, we distinguish first characters from barbarous forms conjoined with those first (as in Egyptian hieroglyphics[2]), leaving only the beautiful anaglyphics (relief-works

in use—in 1000—have been employed to the use of First characters and barbarously mixed with those (as by the Egytians).   But scarcely without design of mystery, a priesthood, and (as is notorious in that case) magic, etc.   And even by the hieroglyphics [of the Egyptians] it appears in their mixture with other notes and characters (which are of no imitation, after life, or natural shapes, but purely characters of the first kind as Arabic, Chinese, etc.) that the way of first characters was known to them, and that the other so much boasted way was but an abridgment or concealment of these: an art superinduced, and afterwards regulated, prescribed, and maintained ceremoniously, rationally, orthodoxly, and specifically, as said below p. 125 latter part.

[1] Of which the cause see below, p. 125.

[2] After the middle or third sort of characters and hieroglyphics thus fully discussed (with account in passing of Egyptian priesthood, mystery, as here and p. 125), subjoin Oxford Almanac as among examples, "which for ugliness of figures etc., might pass as truly mystic, priestly and hieroglyphic; but otherwise emblematic, or at least so aimed, and the third or middle order intended."   Appellation, viz. "Those famous academical anaglyphics, of annual edition—emblematic nostradamus's of the age of Christian church renowned for prophecies in church and state.

So many pretty cubs of mice and moles handed about, penny-books, together with almanac and prayer-books; cried in the street by the fat man with strutting body and big voice.

Orthodox forms (as the Egyptians above), so these Oxford, awkward figures.   So the originals, viz. doctors, college men, etc." Raillery.

and inwrought of the polite ancients) as a true species of art and workmanship: in the emblematic way. But this also being slightly touched and explained, we pass over to the unmixed, the simple and pure, viz. "design, plastic art; second, poetry, imagery, iconography, typography (improperly applied to printing characters), by type, prototype and ectype; and the just imitation of nature according to natural history and the ideas or species of the several forms, animal or vegetative, to some end and with some intent." E.g. In a single figure of a human body: "A man. Why? What man?" Answer: "A strong man." Therefore here something learnt.—"A beautiful well-made man." Again something learnt.—"An ugly, cruel, dangerous man." Therefore caution, discernment[1] taught; the mind profited, advanced; and fancy, judgment improved; knowledge of the species, of our own species, of *ourselves*, the best and chief knowledge, a step hither. So all imitation of natural things according to the great master in his Poetics.

Nothing being more pleasant to human nature from the beginning as this learning, viz. This is this[2]: distinguishing into species and classes (the way to record, remember, lay up, draw consequences), and helping society, and communion of thought and sense; information mutual, delightful. Mimicry of the better sort. All men *mimic*, else no speech, no manners. And hence the Egyptians made a monkey

---

[1] Physiognomy and penetration into tempers, manners, designs (the dark cabinet), as far as natural and true is learnt also by this art from the ideas of the great masters. See below, p. 100.

[2] Hic ille est. ὁ αὐτοῦ, *Demosthenes*. Digito monstrari et dicier hic est. *Pers*. Sat. I, 28. Who is the *ille*? Some pre-science, else nothing learnt. Thus in the imitative poetic part of painting and plastic art, reference (in the higher sense) to the innate idea of forms as explained above, viz....; and (in the lower sense) to the early learnt species or general classes, the natural sort, into which nature has actually and necessarily cast, as into moulds, the severally organised creatures and their generations successive. As, "This is a horse!" How like! "This a dog, a water-dog, a land-spaniel, a hound!" etc. So a child delighted (according to Aristotle's *Poetics*, IV.). Something learnt.

the hieroglyphic of learning, and modern painters use it for universities[1].

2. CHARACTERS, PERSONAGES.

Second Characters (viz. with regard to the title[2]) are *moral* personal personages.

See the chief verse and hinge of Horace's poetic art (vers. 86) Descriptas servare vices, operumque colores, i.e. χαρακτῆρας et mores in dramatico [" To observe the distinctions described and the complexion of works," i.e. characters and the customs in the dramatic]. I.e. Actionum affectuum humanorum in scenis ubi res agitur (ut Hor. *de arte poet.* vers. 179) in satyra refertur tantum quare. [Of the affects of human actions on the stage where the affair is acted out only so much is related in satire as....] Sic Isocrates ad Demonicum, χαρακτῆρα τοῖς ἔργοις ἐπιβάλλειν [to stamp characters upon deeds]. Et Demosth. ἐν δὲ ταῖς ὁμιλίαις ὁ τῆς ψυχῆς χαρακτὴρ βλέπεται [but in intercourse the character of the soul is seen]. Sic rursus infra de comedia Hor. *De arte poet.* v. 156 Aetatis cujusque etc. Mobilibusque decor naturis [of every age etc. and to changing tempers a proper decorum]. *Vide* Hor. *Sat.* lib. 1. vers. 12 Defendente vicem modo rhetoris, atque poetae ["maintaining the character now of the orator, and now of the poet"]. Et *infra, De arte poet.* vers. 193, Officiumque virile defendat [and perform the duty manfully]. Partes defendere idem quod hic servare vices [to perform

---

[1] See "Iconologia" di Cesare Ripa upon the word *accademia*: "Il cinocefalo ovvero babbuino lo faciamo assistente dell' accademia per essere egli stato tenuto dagli egitu ieroglifico de le lettere, e pero lo consecrauano a mercurio repartato, inventore et autore di tutte le lettere si come riferisce." Pierio Valeriano, 'Hieroglyphica,' Venet. 1604 lib. VI, p. 38.

All this premised that the following chapters, phrases, terms, etc. may be easy, viz. Second characters. Signature. Designation. Inwroughts. Typography etc., the fixed and settled terms or expressions for notions as just above. So much therefore as to this, now proceed.

[2] *Supra*, p. 1.

the parts as likewise to preserve here the changes].
Sic Hor. *Epist.* I. lib. 2, vers. 171, Partes tutetur
[supports the character].

> Quisquis erit vitae, scribam, color.
>
> Horace. *Sat.* I. lib. II. v. 60.

[Whatever be the colour of my life, I will write.]

Again Horace, *de arte poetica*, vers. 101–113

> Ut ridentibus arrident, ita flentibus adsunt
> Humani vultus...
>   male si mandata loqueris,
> Aut dormitabo, aut ridebo. Tristia maestum
> Vultum verba decent...
> Format enim natura prius non intus ad omnem
> Fortunarum habitum:...
> Si dicentis erunt fortunis absona dicta,
> Romani tollent equites peditesque cachinnum.

["As the human countenance smiles on those that
smile, so does it sympathize with those that weep....

If you pronounce the parts assigned you ill, I shall
either fall asleep or laugh.

Pathetic accents suit a melancholy countenance....

For nature forms us first to every modification of
fortune...

If the words be discordant to the station of the
speaker, the Roman knights and plebeians will raise an
immoderate laugh." Smart.]

The same ridicule as when even a Guido makes
his Andromeda dance (Lord Devon's picture) though
chained and in sight of the monster.

The truth of the affections:

> Aetatis cujusque notandi sunt tibi mores,
> Mobilibusque decor naturis dandus et annis.
>
> HOR. *de arte poet.* v. 156.

["The manners of every age must be marked by
you, and a proper decorum assigned to men's varying
dispositions and years."]

Imberbis juvenis v. 161 ["the beardless youth"].
Semper in adjunctis, aevoque morabimur aptis.
v. 178.
["We must dwell always upon those qualities which
are joined and adapted to each person's age."]
Thus also the painter's science and wisdom, knowledge of men and things, moral characters, etc.
...ille profecto
Reddere personae scit convenientia cuique,
Respicere exemplar[1] vitae morumque jubebo
Doctum imitatorem, et veras hinc ducere voces.
...morataque recte
Fabula...   v. 315—319.
["He certainly knows how to give suitable attributes
to every character. I should direct the learned imitator
to have a regard to the mode of nature and manners,
and thence draw his expressions to the life...A play
where the manners are well marked."]

Ficta voluptatis causa sint proxima veris,
Nec quodcunque volet, poscat sibi fabula credi.
v. 338-9.
["Let whatever is imagined for the sake of entertainment, have as much likeness to truth as possible; but
whatever it chooses, let not your play demand belief."]
Which is the same as the incredulous ode[2] (v. 188)
cited already in the Notion.
Hence metamorphoses dangerous subjects, though
so common with moderns.
Quere. Whether any subject, and how managed
by the ancients. Just painters. Answer...[3]

[1] Good in Socraticis chartis habet (*ut supra*, v. 310) ubi person et
characteres, moras nimiarum quia dialogi erant. *Vide* Aristot. *Poet.*,
cap. I (Σωκράτικος λόγοι), *Athenaeum*, lib. II.
[2] Refer hence to Charac-cks, vol. III, p. 181. Note Vitruvius.
[3] Note. Remember in this place dialogue writing, imitative,
political, dramatic, active. Drawing and design as in Moralists, II, 187:
"To lay colours," etc. and moral painting (all true painting being moral)
in the following page, viz. 188.
Also what is said at length of dialogue ·drawing and design etc. in
Miscellany etc. See Index there and particularly vol. I, pp. 201, 202.

...Sibi convenientia finge. v. 119.
["Frame new characters which with themselves shall well accord."]

The Characters which in poetry are included in the 5th and last part (according to Horace's concealed division in his *Ars Poet.*) answer, in painting to the symmetry and proportion of the figures. Because suppose a hand or head given, the rest of the figure must answer this species. For there are such and such: and these the painter must investigate from observation and instinct. A Moor in the East and a West-Indian, not only different in colours, hair, feature, but whole proportion. And even among Europeans: a Swede, Dane, Briton, how different even from Flemish, and High-German, much more from Spaniard, Gascon, or South Frenchman. The Huns, (Gothic invaders from the East and North-East parts of Europe) how described[1], resembling the present Tartars, short-necked, squat, square, and something peculiar about the head and nose.

Thus particular symmetry (viz. the figures and forms) are in the Characters; since these in poetry are included in the moral part, or manners. For manners are here properly exhibited by characters only, their opposition, contrast, foil, operation : whence the purgation spoken of by Aristotle and explained in Char-cks[2].

The didactive or preceptive way being un-artificial, un-masterly, and un-poetic : not Homerical, though Virgilian. This the province of the philosopher, the rhetorician, the historian : not the bard, the *vates*, the enthusiast. Thus Sophocles more poetical than even Euripides, though the latter refined beyond him and excelled in style and other parts ; particularly in sentences in which this moral irregularity and encroachment on the philosophers or rhetoricians part so much the better afforded him scope.

---

[1] Quere. Where find it ?
[2] Vol. III, p. 262. Notes, line 17.

Corollarily. That particular division of the five in painting called symmetry (viz. of the figures with respect to themselves) is separate and abstract from the moral part and manners; which in poetry includes characters and mental forms. On the other hand, the moral part in painting lies but little in the forms (for Socrates, a Silenus whom he resembled, a triton, the centaur Chiron, or any other less specious form corporeal may be principally moral), but is expressed in the air, feature, attitude, action, motion; and is therefore wholly lodged in that part of painting called the movements, where action, passion, the affections are shown. Thus Characters which in painting are mere forms are not moral, though in poetry always moral and belonging to ethics in that division[1].

Again. "What is it we see? A boy—therefore, sweet, pretty, innocent: But a cupid. A new case. A boy and beautiful boy, the most that is possible; but not innocent, not harmless, not wholly sweet, gentle, loving: but mischievous, treacherous, mocking, subtle. An urchin, half civil, demon, cruel, spiteful, proud, disdainful, tyrannical, capricious, imperious[2]." Here a new story, a new lesson, an instruction[3], something learnt. For wretched would be that painter, who being to paint a cupid, or several cupids, should lose this essential moral part. No history, no true form, no cupid[4], if this be lost: if this visibly appear not and the manners, character preserved according to the poetic idea and hypothesis. This is *plastic* truth. And this in Ascanius (when truly Ascanius) very different from a cupid, when the habit and form of Ascanius, but

---

[1] At this place under the black line begins the division of this head (occasioned by the equivocal word Characters): viz. into Characters 1st, 2d, 3d (as hitherto above ever since, p. 90) and into characters of life, manners etc., which begins at this paragraph occasionally drawn from what preceded.

[2] Compare place with Char-cks, vol. III, p. 319.

[3] So again below, p. 101.

[4] Mem^d. Here in Sig^n Porchinaro's collection at Naples, his two cupids, the one of Jacint Prandi, the other Sig^n Parli; the first good style, but character lost; the latter French style and air, but character kept. The former, however, preferred (is bought because of the practise etc.).

carrying his own *true* manner and character; which it would be curious in an able painter to preserve in this history, if it were to be represented by a great hand. Quite otherwise as to cupid when he is out of his natural character and form, as in the story of Psyche, where not only his size is manly and form different, but history and manner altered, character changed: a party and concerned himself; a sufferer under his other self; a patient, an actor; not a god or demon, or genius, in the machine part and superior roll of a deity invested in his proper powers and habits, arts, practices, etc. See Raphael (so judicious!) on this subject, in the Vatican[1].

Explanation, viz. the 5th part in painting called "*symmetry* is abstract from the moral part, which lies chiefly in the air, feature &c. and in the movements[2], where action, passion, and the affections." Add "in some measure also in the custom[3], habit, dress, helping the air and describing the manners."

And here insert "the different describers (poets and painters) of the better and worse humanity, according to Aristotle's Poetics...where such and such a one (viz....) described them better; such and such a one (viz....) worse."

And here dividing and distinguishing between the heroic and lower, or 3rd comic (to which the ryparographers[4] answer) a word or two of these latter in as far only as they are characteristical, therefore pleasing by a *je ne sais quoi*, which is easily explained. As among other[5] instances remember the modern common

---

[1] If not there, on the walls.   [2] Viz. of 4th part.
[3] Viz. of 1st part.   [4] *Infra*, p. 136.
[5] La Bruyère (after Théophraste) the chief. And here remember not only to cite and comment on a few principal characters, but (in the notes still) transcribe his whole passage of ancient and modern manners in his preface. And remember his French court at mass, their backs to the God they worship (their altar and god-wafer), and faces to the tribunal, i.e. the king. Long perukes, etc.
See also what may be inserted here in the text itself (without scruple of self-citation, as resolved above, p. 4) concerning Characteristics from vol. I, p. 201 etc., viz. "Such or such a face, etc. Every face must be a certain man's."

author, our guest Mon^r St Evremond, one of his
best things (slighting the rest) is his exact copy
after the life of the old French Marshall de —— and
the Jesuit.   So an Italian, or Spaniard, an odd figure
wrapt in a ragged cloak, but with formal mien,
the shrug, or strut.   So a country peasant, or boor,
a Jew.   One of Salvator Rosa's cut-throat figures,
shaberoons, ragamuffins, moss-troopers, knights of the
post, jilts, drabs, eavesdroppers, gamesters, sharks,
players, musicians, mountebanks, quack doctors,
sharpers, *ambubaiarum collegia.*
All these the more pleasing as more secret,
mysterious, difficult and withal instructive in manners,
and of real use in life, and towards the knowledge of
mankind and the world.   And upon this found this
maxim or rule, viz. : " That in all such satirical characteristics, as the finer and better subjects of imitation,
are the more concealed and not the obvious, staring,
notorious faults in manners.   So the finer and more
delicate imitation is the more tender, and by nicest
slightest touches in poetry as in painting, and not by
exaggeration, amplification, straining, tightening, over-
charging."   (Caricature, burlesque in one kind, bom-
bast and gigantic in the other.)   On which very thing
depends the difference between Horace and Juvenal.
Sordidus et luscus qui possit dicere lusce.   [Sordid and
half blind the man who can speak blindly.]   So a
sordid painter first chooses a mean blemish and not a
true one in manners : and then withal exaggerates.
A blind fiddler instead of Tigellinus, a king's chapel...:
debaucher of youth, rake, dissolute and gamester, etc.
Remember also our Shakespeare's Jack Falstaff;
a character.   And here indeed the form itself helps
the manners.   But overdone and spoilt both by poet
and players.   The painter (a Salvator Rosa and
tolerable good satirist in poetry) would not hyperbole[1]

[1] Not in his little perspective figures, though in heroic often guilty, and
even in perspective for horror's sake.

so; but moderate the hyperbole[1] and strike the imagination far better.

Remember also Voiture's delight in his letters from Spain of the scenes of Don Quixote where he was travelling. Strange impression of character.

Something therefore there is in every design, or designatory work of imitation, and copy after nature (be it even in animals, fruit, or flower-pieces), which answers to the history in a truly epic or poetic work. This is in truth and strictness historical, moral, *characteristic*. The note or character of nature, the form, natural habit, constitution, reason of the thing, its energy, operation, place, use or effect in nature : if ill and mischievous to us, that we may record and avoid ; if salutary, record and improve. This is the moral, the intelligence of the fable. "Such a one he is! You see him in his true colours! This is the man! Such he is—*Sic, Crito est hic!* As in the Roman comic poet[2], so in the animal, beast or fowl. This is the creature! Such he is! Be it a lion. See how like! Such is his easy march, his unconcernedness, his want of fear, his consciousness of mastery, superiority, and his contempt of other creatures. Such his slowness and largeness, though ready for activity and agility, when roused by any assault or called by hunger to his prey.—Is it a bull[3]? See the same grum indifference,

---

[1] Of the hyperbole see below, p. 154.

[2] Andrea, Act V, Sc. 4, *supra*, p. 93.

[3] Thus the animal, but chiefly the cattle-painter, not so easily the bird-man. The horse belonging to humanity and history, to be studied by the great master, so noble a creature he is and so near human nature in the expression of passion, etc., so fitted to man. Thus I say, the animal painters of the comic order (as cock and dung-hill) become historian, poetic.

A whole. (1) Unity of spirit in the kind, harmony of the sexes, economy, the young, the old, the bell-wether, the master, reverend, long-bearded, longsbard goat, the ram.

The seraglio, grand-seignior, and concubines of the place. (2) Unity of the group or groups, a principal figure, etc., with all the other rules.

On the contrary, an unable artist or one guided by the bespeaker (these being a poor mean race), and turned out of his way (which though unable to give the reason, he would and often does naturally and by taste alone pursue) when the group is finished the animal nature, action, sullen security and ease, trust to his strength, the jealousy of his eye over his females on the approach of anything injurious to them, or any rivalship from his own kind.—Is it a bird ? A tame one merely, and of the household kind ? A cock ? See his walk, his *démarche*, his carriage amongst his ladies ; his generosity, even to the starving himself and neglect of his own sustenance !"

The courage of all these creatures, their ready exposing of their lives in the defence of their kind! The tractableness and tameness of these! The unsubduable, indomitable fierceness, and love of liberty in the others! The tenderness and innocence of some! the savageness and cruelty of others!—The *characteristic* still, the truth, the historic is all in all, and the τὸ φυσικὸν, the τὸ.... The thing *imitated*, the thing *specified* (reduced to its true form and species) is all in all, the whole delight, pleasure of the work, the secret charm of the spectacle. This accomplished and all is done. Instruction, moral description, truth.

The meaning, the intelligence, humour, thought. A sense. A thought. Even in portraiture[1], as a statue of a senator (nature concurring, and the person being in shape and feature adapted). This is a sense, a thought. Even an indifferent person, etc. So a promising youth, hero, prince, etc. *Quantum instar ipso est !*[2] [Whatever the form exactly is.]

humour shown in its simplicity and agreeable truth. He unhappily introduces *a man* (humanity spoiling all), or else an inferior or foreign nature, or some way incoherent, as a peacock with the cock and hens, and something like this in a beautiful group of cattle by the heat under a shade by a pool's side, and casting the spectator into an agreeable revery†.

† Remember in this place to improve this description of the summer heat and cattle attempted, as in a forest or wild common, to a shade of trees and water, the flies fled from, and cattle for coolness in the water, tails playing. Nothing of this view (if broken by foreign figures) capable of bestowing that sweet revery.

[1] Portraiture, *infra*, p. 134.   [2] Virgil's *Aeneid*, VI, 865.

3. RISE, PROGRESS, DECLENSION AND REVIVAL OF SECOND CHARACTERS[1].

Politeness in figures helped still to polish grace. So music. But Plato and other philosophers and sages look wistfully towards the Egyptian laws (as lovers of rarities for such the Athenians, such the Greeks in general, and so humoured even by a Xenophon) admiring mystery, hiding secrets from the vulgar. This, as being frighted by the popular spirit, felt so severely in the person of their master Socrates. Besides Plato's and Pythagoras' affectation of legis- latourship and pulse beating towards that noble ambition, to which the first a sacrifice and the second often tempted, and in state affairs under Dion brought in considerable danger. Hence his emulation with Homer, envious and somewhat detracting way, too truly objected by Dionysius Halicarnassus.

True indeed that by this ungenerous and hierar- chical polity the state of longer duration[2]. For of what duration Egypt? But then what a state! What barbarity! Superstition! And when enervated once: how perpetual a slavery, from Mede and Persian, to Marmaluke and Turk.

Insinuation from hence, as to the last and present grand hierarchy of Romish Church. Whether not

[1] Quere from Herodotus, Diodorus Siculus…: Marsham, etc., about the records of the Egyptians: how far back. Hierarcho-political reason, as below, p. 125 for retaining the first ancient and hieroglyphic forms and statues of the gods, etc.

[2] Proof of this from the hierarchical policy and hope always to engage sovereign and bring over and reconcile even the conqueror partly by superstition (sin and pleasure), partly by policy as assistant to him. Hence easy betrayer of their national form, prince and people. Trust to spiritual weapons for their own preservation at least (come what will of nobles, prince or people), as when Attila was met and Alexander by the Jewish priests (see Arrianus). Hence the oracles (though a Grecian and much limited priesthood) after they had stood steady all along, yet when things desperate and almost all Greece conquered, (Athens not resisting but driven to sea), began to faint and preach submission. This Herodotus saw and honestly noted. Though for this and other freedoms, i.e. poetic liberty as complaining of the gods, lashed by honest Plutarch, himself a priest.

better to have followed the Egyptian in this (as in many other things) and keep the orthodox forms horrid, savage, and consequently inspiring superstition, as in reality their first were from the Gothic times or last feces of the Empire and of Arts, when images, etc., were introduced.

And though Protestants take the contrary weapon (and very justly from the present period), yet for the larger and more extensive period of time. Quere. Whether this may not weaken and supplant, as it polishes and refines, *emollit mores.* Nothing more true in nature can be said. So chiefly a fine picture or statue frontispiece, a fine piece of music, effeminacy indeed, an evil consequent : but not necessarily so, if the magistrate provides, without totally banishing (as Lycurgus some sorts of music and most arts, because of his local and specific commonwealth), or prohibiting as Plato in the case of Homer.

Therefore as beauteous forms polish (taking politeness with its consequences), so ugly barbarise[1]. None impossible ; or if practicable, still equally barbarous.

Moses (*non obstante* 2d commandment) raised a serpent, and after him the arch and *sànctus sanctorum,* their cherubs, etc., the brazen tree, its buds, etc.

Prohibition therefore such as Egyptian, Jewish, (or suppose Scythian or Persian), and absolute abhorrence of figure or temple, a savage and barbarising enthusiasm.

Apology and protestation against entering into the decision of the Egyptian and Chinese pretensions to antiquity (so far beyond Moses') in their records[2], though recite the authorities. But this assert : that neither Jew, Egyptian, nor Chinese polite.

This a judgment of politeness. If polite : show me a picture, a statue, coin, proportion, nature. But arabesque ! Japan ! Indian ! Savage. Monstrous.

---

[1] *Infra,* p. 123.   [2] *Supra,* p. 103.

Even in their portraiture, pleasure-pieces, wanton pieces. Also gods monstrous, frightful according to Egyptian[1] and Syrian models; or Turkish mosques, no architecture, or statuary, or figures : or as bad as none.

Frightful, horrid, cruel ideas entertained, advanced by such divine forms; soft, gentle, humane ideas, by truly human forms, and divinity represented after the best, sweetest, and perfectest idea of humanity to the vulgar. But without application to divinities, and simply viewed and contemplated in cities, groves, high-ways, places, gardens, forums, etc., *emollit mores*.

"Bad figures: bad minds." "Crooked designs: crooked fancies." "No designs : no thought." So Turks, etc. "No imitation : no poetry." No arts of this kind : no letters, or at least in a poor degree. So politeness always holds proportion with laws and liberty. So that where the one is with a tolerable progress in the first species (viz. 1st Characters), the other (viz. 2d Characters) will soon prevail. And where it ceases and tyranny (such as the Eastern monarchies, ancient and modern) prevails, art and 2d Characters accordingly sink. See Japan! Mogul! China! Turk and Tartar! Show me amongst their infinite delicacy of other work a single 2d Character, a *form*, even but a single figure a perspective, a statue, coin, palace, architecture—that is not worse than Gothic. Show but so much as a vase ! till in China taught by us and the Dutch.

4. INSTINCT, NATURAL IDEAS, ETC.

Those philosophers (modern) the poorest and most shifting, for the sake of a system, hypothesis, who, surpassing all ancient conceits and extravagances of the kind, deny ideas, sense, perception, (i.e. life) to animals. But those yet poorer and more shifting, who impugn natural ideas and ridicule instinct and innate

[1] *Infra*, p. 125.

ideas, because perhaps abused, misapplied, carried too
far by some modern preceding writers, or by Plato.

The same philosophers would confound the very
notion of species, specific ideas (sad virtuosos!)[1]. But
had not the creatrix or sovereign plastic nature set the
boundaries, the caprice (i.e. wantonness and bestiality)
of corrupt man would long since have gone beyond
any of the worst painters, grotesque ῥυπάρογράφοι, etc.
as well beyond any of the poets in composing new
complicated forms of satires, etc., with which the breed
would have run out and been lost. But now even in
the inward, several species (within the genus) as in
dogs and fowls, which breed with one another, a natural
propensity for like joining with like ; so that the breed
when mixed and blended, in time and after several
consequent generations displays and opens itself, and
the orders return to their first natural secretions, purity
and simplicity of form[2].

An ingenious author and notable metaphysician[3]
about twenty years ago took such an advantage from
the affected fulsome and common use of instinct and
innate ideas, that being extremely well received and
heard on account of his excellent genius and capacity
in other writings, these words grew so out of fashion
that a man of sense durst hardly use them on the most
proper and most obvious occasion. And it was safer
for a gentleman who was a lover of sports to say
seriously upon the subject of his chase, that his dog,
jowler, or tomboy reasoned or meditated, than that he
had *natural sagacity* or *instinct*. We were allowed,
indeed, to say that the poor turner's pot had sense and
feeling above the iron-jack which supplied his room,

---

[1] See M^cC.

[2] Memorandum. Room here for demonstration of the young swallow.
First flight precipitated, viz. from a rock over the sea, or an eminence
over a paved court, or place fatal to fall. Yet the equilibrium instantly
found and the art known, not learnt. Strength only failing when supported by the old ones, not art wanting. To the birds' nest, as well or
better, more exact the first than afterwards as in Charac-ks, vol. II,
pp. 307, 411, 412, etc.

[3] The same as above.

(for Cartesianism was not admitted in its strict sense). But it was dangerous to talk of breeds, either of dogs, or hogs, or horses, lest we should betray our ignorance in imagining according to the vulgar error, that passions, affections, instincts, inclinations, impressions, impulses, ideas, imaginations (ready for the object when prescribed, and even raising or calling up a feigned and false object when the season or ripeness came) should possibly be delivered down in descent and extract to particular species. Nay even the species themselves were called in question, and more than called in question, flatly denied.

As thus poor Horace and other poets, even in their epicurean and least theological fits, were very credulous and superstitious and foolish, when they said for instance :

Est in juvencis...patrum virtus[1].

[The merit of the sire survives in the offspring.]

The *rictus* and gapings of noxious creatures, bears, lions, wolves, crocodiles, dragons, even small serpents and insects (as vipers) imprinted, previous mould or sockets to speak by analogy (as no other way in cases of sensation, intelligence, perception, egoity, not confined to place or determined by it).

So on the other hand who can doubt the contraries, viz. beauteous faces (especially in the same kind) to be equally imprinted by innate characters, moulds, preparatory sockets for reception and recognition of such joyous forms, as in the passion between the sexes.

Who would charge human nature with this dullness and so readily clear and acquit the bestial ? unless perhaps the senseless modern philosophy and fool hypothesis of insensibility be brought in play for cavil's sake.

What more certain than that the poorest ignoramus of our species, being kept from seeing anything but

[1] Horace's *Carmina*, Lib. iv, Ode IV, l. 30.

old males, and clothed bodies (as in monkish cloister, or barbarous hermitage) would in a clear light, when brought to see nudities, distinguish between the true and natural, and the unnatural deformed kind.

Thus the species of horses and other animals, the kind being once seen and nature helped (changes not seen in perfection, but far off), the idea of beauty and perfection is raised, and when reduced to this idea of instinct by the able artist, recognised presently by the good eye of every spectator.

If a female of our own species (to pass by the love of babies and that shrewd propensity) should after a great belly got she scarce knew how, not find herself inclined to pick straws, or make a nest: no wonder, because of the second string to the bow, reason, discourse, community, the reserve[1]. Nor is it a wonder any more, that coming to lose the same great belly, and the season at hand for suckling, etc., that she has not the *conatus* or effort, that she calls not for the babies newly left off, nor does what is answerable to the hen, bustling about, swelling her wings, stretching her legs, picking and scraping like a thing mad and in fury.

5.   Taste, Relish, Eye, Judgment, Criticism.

1.   Pedantry in painting, as in scholarship, mere scholar, mere painter ; colleges of scholars, academies of painters.

Seldom a thorough, practising, labouring scholar, not a pedant. Seldom an orator, a poet; but seldomer, hardly ever a painter. Yet sometimes a Homer (if we may judge by a guess), sometimes a Horace, a Xenophon, a Demosthenes, a Socrates, an Apelles, a Raphael.

2.   First corruption of taste, from bad sculptures, prints, etc., and drawing without masters. For so in all other exercises, as fencing, dancing, etc. Better

[1] As in ' Moralists,' p. 307.

never have learnt. Ask all masters. Appeal to all able. For habits not to be broken. Besides conceit gains, and stiffness ; or surfeit contracted, and aversion to the study and science. Ungrateful because unsuccessful. Hence pedantry in petty virtuosos. Gentry lose their taste and exchange for a worse than mere painters. Second corruption. Haste, hurry. Therefore arts contemplatory require *otium* ; thrive only (as letters and philosophy) where much of this recess from public. Yet a public and activity, i.e. action carrying on, debates, freedom, liberty, etc. Soliloquy[1] necessary here as in philosophy[2].

[1] See 'Soliloquy' in ' Characteristics.'
[2] Second Corruption. See Junius' *de pictura veterum*, Lib. I. c. 5, p. 34. In pursuance of soliloquy referred to[1]. " Nihil est curiosius otiosis." Plinius Jun. *Epist.* 32, Lib. IX. " Frequentia et obambulatio hominum conturbat et infirmat imaginum notas : solitudo conservat integras simulacrorum figuras." Cornificius, *Rhet. ad Herenn.* Lib. III, xix. Quamobrem etiam recte Plinius, agens de ea tranquillitate animi et securitate otii quae debetur harum artium considerationi. Magni officiorum negotiorumque acervi inquit abducunt omnes a contemplatione talium ; quoniam otiosorum et in magno loci silentio apta admiratio talis est. In promptu est ratio: phantasiam enim, cujus in diligenti artis inspectione praecipuae partes sunt, vacuus animus et sola tacentiaque loca mirifice excitant atque alunt. Quumque perfectum, accuratumque picturarum admiratorem veras omnium rerum species animo concipere, conceptasque ad examinanda pulcherrimae artis experimenta advocare oporteat, manifestum etiam est neutrum horum sine virtute imaginativa effici posse ; ac ne ipsam quidem imaginum conformationem[2], quotidianis negotiis et discurrentium tumultu interpellatam, bene procedere. Videas itaque cultores artis minime vanos, si forte aliquando liberiores et magis vacuos ab interventoribus dies nacti sunt, nunquam non per otium adsuefacere animos absolutissimis quibusque rerum imaginibus colligendis atque in animum congerendis. Atque hoc est illud quod ait Apollonius apud Philostratum, Lib. II, cap. XXII. Τοὺς ὁρῶντας τὰ τῆς γραφικῆς ἔργα, μιμητικῆς δεῖσθαι οὐ γὰρ ἂν ἐπαινέσειέ τις τὸν γεγραμμένον ἵππον ἢ ταῦρον, μὴ τὸ ζῷον ἐνθυμηθείς, ᾧ εἴκασται. Eos, qui pictoriae artis opera inspiciunt, indigere imaginativa facultate. Nemo enim recte laudaverit pictum equum, nisi qui animal illud animo concipiat, cujas similitudinem pictura exprimit ; vide locum. Inspice quoque Platonem Lib. II, de Legibus. Quamvis autem ratio haec, quam attulimus, solitudinem satis commendet artificum opera dijudicaturis ; praesto tamen est et alia non minus praegnans, quae idem suadeat. Quemadmodum enim medicis non apparentia modo

[1] *Nat. Hist.* Lib. XXXVI, cap. v.
[2] Compare this contemplative habit with the truly contemplative and mental to which this leads, and of which it borrows when refined and improved in right virtuosoship, etc. Compare I say with Maximus Tyrius (as in little black paper book, p. 8).

Third corruption. Vice, corruption itself, prostitution. Worse sort of ῥυπάρογράφοι, viz. obscene acts, very deformity. Hence in a second degree not quite so lewd, effeminacy (as expressed in the last paragraph of the Notion), the licked manner, *leché* in French; the enamelled, the very paint (as Flemish phrase), just as if it were painted.

Fourth corruption (or rather prevention, deprivation). Want of nudity, statuary, distortion of bodies[1], etc.

Painter's taste like dancing masters[2] in carriage. All towards the affectation. Quite contrary to the ancient. All modern. No ancient (not of the worst workmen) guilty of this, because of the many models extant, which though ill copied, yet no new designed after the affected way (the *sweer* as they call it). Raphael never guilty of this; nor Poussin, though a Frenchman.

Quere. About Raphael's admired figure of the

vitia notanda sunt, verum etiam invenienda qua latent; saepe ipsis, qui sanandi sunt, ea occulentibus : ita ad inspiciendas picturas admissus, plura, quam prima facie ostendi videntur, rimabitur; cujus rei in solitudine certius judicium; quod in turba spectantibus frequenter aut suus cuique favor, aut ille laudantium clamor extorquet. Pudet enim dissentire, et velut tacita quadam verecundia inhibemur plus nobis credere; cum interim et vitiosa pluribus placeant, et ab adulantibus laudentur etiam quae non placent; cum denique optime pictis gratiam pravia judicia non referant.

Quotquot igitur huic curae sedulo incumbere in animum inducunt, de industria quandoque sumunt certas quasdam imagines, quas quam numerosissime versent, velut eadem cera aliae atque aliae formae duci solent. Plastae certe atque ii qui coloribus utuntur, ex ipsis rebus capessunt notiones quibus lineamenta, lucem, umbram, eminentias, recessus imitentur. In singulis corporibus praestantissimas quasque verae pulchritudinis notas observant, easque in unum aliquod opus conferunt; ut non tam didicisse a natura, quam cum ea certasse, aut potius illi legem dedisse videantur. Quis enim putet ullam unquam talem fuisse foeminae cujusquam pulchritudinem, in qua nihil desideraret non vulgaris judex? Nam tametsi in ipsis naturae normis atque dimensionibus universa perfectio est; tamen utriusque parentis mistio, tempus, coelum, locus, improvisus aliquis casus, et vaga quaevis cogitatio naturali formae non nihil possunt detrahere similitudinum quidem in mente reputatio est, inquit Plinius *Nat. Hist.* Lib. VII, cap. 12. et in qua credantur multa fortuita pollere; visus, auditus, memoria, haustaeque imagines sub ipso conceptu, etc.

¹ See below, p. 117.   ² *Infra*, p. 128.

sitting woman (Justice) and the ostrige? Esteemed
the finest (by painters), to me seems the most modern
and ergo...
Criticism. How necessary here; as in other arts
according to Char-cks.
Horace's reason:

Ut pictura poesis erit; quae, si...
           —volet haec sub luce videri,
Judicis argutum quae non formidat acumen.
Haec placuit semel: haec decies repetita placebit[1].

["As with a painting so with a poem; one...another
will prefer to brave the open light, dreading not the
critics keenest skill: this pleases once; this viewed ten
times will please."]
If this were true in nature (as I would not give
credit, because of founding no argument on hypo-
thetical, or dubious foundation, but on fact and truth)
here would be a high commendation indeed of ideas,
imagery, and the force of the $\phi a \nu \tau a \sigma i a \iota$, fleeting forms[2],
etc. Not only our painters but our women should
imagery, etc. (treat this in raillery) for fear of the breed.
Caution against prejudice, prevention, prepos-
session from artificial and half-taste, gathered from
painters or empirical and practical science (the worst
imaginable) in gentlemen.
As thus:
A parallel, since such are fashionable, between
painting and eloquence, rhetoric, etc. (as often between
that and poetry). "O pulchrum prosopopeiam" (as in
Petronius) so here. "O the fine fore-shortening!"
Thus in pulpit rhetoric and priest-oratory, at a
country church especially, or in a college among the
bearded boys and pedants. "O the excellent turn,
application of the Greek sentence! O the division!
quotation!" So in French (Moliere's comedy) "si bien
que je n'entendais goutte."

[1] Hor. *de Arte Poet.* ll. 361—5.
[2] As below, p. 143.

Reasons why a gentleman's taste if practical and empirical[1] necessarily false :

First Reason. Becomes interested, makes himself a party, espouses a manner, style, mannerist in lowest degree and below the painter by trade and profession. Also judge and party in the cause unfair. So Nero's[2] voice and acting (remember Agrippinus, etc.) in the divine man, and so again the governour of the Grecian province and the people differing about the actor or advice.

Dilemma. Either has an idea or not. If an idea : a hand to come up to it or not. If a hand obedient and answering, then a painter *omnibus numeris*; if a hand inferiour unanswering, then being not obliged to pursue as a professor, or for maintenance, but wholly voluntary and for pleasure only, must lose his end, and hate his products. For if loves and pleasure come by degrees, through self love, conceit, or flattery ; then here comes the corruption, here the taste inevitably miscarries, grows awry, warps, turns crooked, perverse. Carry this reasoning into music[3].

Second Reason. Extravagant fondness for *one* master, *one* particular hand, *one* piece (a hundred to one, if a good one). Besides that, no one master yet of the moderns after Raphael has deserved anything like this ; and even as to Raphael see reasons...

So Nero's Greek statue. See Pliny.

Third Reason. That if our gentleman besides his superiour knowledge, learning, education and converse, has not withal a particular genius, idea, and hand superiour to the trading artists and of a degree distinguishable from the common road and style of painting : he must naturally by his study and practice be brought upon a level and familiarized with the set of painters of his time ; and as he is subject to their flattery and emulous of their praise be brought into

---

[1] Exception for gentlemen quite painters as Fabius Pictor.
[2] So also the good emperor Adrian, his great weakness and blemish ; only cause and subject of tyranny in him.
[3] And see below, p. 176.

society and sympathy with this race, so as to be in a manner *one of them*, and of their club and fraternity ; a circumstance which will prove as little advantageous to his fame and reputation as to his manners, his interest, family and estate[1].

The case being the same with this company as with that of players, musicians, songsters, minstrels, dancers, and the rest of those trades and their conspiring crew : all holding together[2].

Nothing even of natural beings worthy of wonder or admiration, but as they show nature's real and highest art, best hand, supreme touches, nature's magnificence, symmetry, proportions, highest orders, supreme order (beyond doric or ionic, beyond corinthian). For what are all these but imitations ? Or as in united and conspiring forms, of actual unity and concurrence in one, means to an end, harmony agreement.

Ergo a tree or even a leaf, beautiful not as a green, not as regularly shaped ; for then a mere turf or cut bush would equal and surpass an old oak, or cedar, or pine. But a rough bit of rock more beautiful in reality than a pearl or diamond. No bribe to make those relished by almost all, and lastingly relished. The other but for a moment, as a rarity, or as set off itself or helping to set off other forms in dress, equipage, etc., of the lowest human caprice and misconception of beauty. Thus grottos, caves, etc., the finest imitations of finest gardening. For this is *truth* ; the rest *false*.

Thus even in nature, the rainbow a mere jewel, an accidental species, refraction, etc. No real *unit*: no being, form, design, end, concurrence. Ergo, a nothing, a non-entity in virtuosoship. A mere miracle or prodigy (without *moral* or *doctrine*) ; a nothing, a juggle. The passion of those who run after monsters in fairies and the θαυμᾰτοποιοί. Prestidigitators.

[1] Mem^d. Exception for Fabius Pictor, etc., as above, p. 112, and the whole man as below, p. 176. Definition of a pedant and how formed in painting, etc., as in other science. Adrian Emperour as above, p. 112.
[2] As said below, p. 176. 'Ambubaiarum collegia.'

Therefore the same here as in life and true wisdom in order to avoid deceit and imposture.

The great business in this (as in our lives, or in the whole of life) is "to correct our taste[1]." For whither will not *taste*[2] lead us? ἀπέχειν, arrest, suspend, defer, delay, proceed gradually, wait, expect, improve... Else we are run away with. The man upon the runaway horse in Lucian's cynic (if so good a piece as that be Lucian's), "Whither away! Whither *this* pleases," viz. his horse, pointing to it. Therefore stop it in its full career, cross it, turn it; and sometimes when lazy even give it the spur; just as in horsemanship, as in breaking the colt.

> Animum rege : qui nisi paret,
> Imperat : hunc frenis, hunc tu compesce catena[3].

["Check your temper, which if not ruled, will sternly rule. Hold it hard in with bit and rein."]

From hence it follows: "That pleasure (in order to reap true pleasure) not to be indulged." Ask, inquire of self. "What sort of pleasure have I? What would I have? Quaere, if the true? if *truth*? to what end? What do I contemplate? What inspect? What to understand, reap, learn[4]?"

Is it to see flesh painted as flesh?—No. This artificial, empirical, the artisan, and even least part of the artisan!—Is it drapery?—No. This of the same kind.—Is it fore-shortnings, academy postures, etc. ?—No. This still empirical.—Is it fine forms in a vicious sense? This false and more so than ever the ryparographics. Since this deforms the beautiful nature; whereas the *cacatorio*, a boor, or soldier, under a hedge or on a dunghill, more nauseating.—Exciting appetite, a horrid reason. Who dares give this for a reason? If so: paint sauces and dishes for the table, smoking pastys, etc. A thought never as yet pursued (I think) any more than curtsying ladies, or bowing

---

[1] *Infra*, p. 144.   [2] τὸ δοκεῖν.
[3] Horat. *Epistola*, Lib. I, Ep. 2, ll. 62, 63.   [4] *Supra*, p. 92.

beaus, except in the French court. Pictures of the pretty princes and princesses, and court-airs as hung in toy shops.

Observe the difference of a right and liberal eye from a mechanic, false: the same in painting and figures, etc., as in real life and *persons*. "What *person*, what form, character, species of a man, do we see? Who was he whom we saw in such a company, in such an action, circumstance, reading, writing, talking, hearkening, musing, exercising?"

A tailor who is asked: he answers (according to his eye). "A gentleman in such a coloured stuff, of such a cut."

If it be a dancing master: he answers (according to his eye). "A gentleman with such a gait or tread, his leg turned so or so."

If it be a fop: he answers (according to his eye) still, and as uniting the two latter tastes. "A gentleman so or so dressed, coming into a room with such or such an air, etc., such coloured lips, such teeth."

But if a man of sense, with an eagle's eye: he answers from his memory and recollection (for so he gathers, collects, imprints, and such is his imagery, history, invention). "A gentleman of such a behaviour, speech, action, such an address, such manners, aspect, and seeming note or character of sense and understanding, temper, mind, soul, and inward complexion."

The artificial, witty, far-fetched, refined, hypercritical taste (what is apt to be commended as ingenuous and merely speculative) is the worst in the world, being half-way, and like half-thinkers (in Char-cks, III, 302). The same in fencing, riding, dancing. The *natural* best, till well and truly formed (see again Char-cks, I, 190, at the end), and the original first rude taste corrected by rule, and reduced to a yet more simple and natural measure. Otherwise an innocent child's eye (of good parts and not spoilt already by pictures of the common sort) always found

the best, as I have found experimentally, in such a one
not of the higher gentry but liberal, and out of the
way of prints, and such costly playthings of imagery,
etc. The same experienced as to likeness in portraiture.

Ergo. Better mere nature than half-way, illa-
borate, artful, merely critical judgment ; as it were in
wantonness, *gayeté de cœur*, with indifference, super-
ciliousness, neglect, scoff, as may be seen even in the
manners, and in the way itself of censuring by these
false-censurers, pseudo critiques, answerable to the
French *pretieuses*, etc.

Better be the mere *je ne sais quoi* of the French.
Though this not in our language : nor I hope ever
will. But for us (I hope) something better reserved.

Docti rationem artis intelligunt, indocti voluptatem[1].

[" The learned understand the art of composition, the
unlearned enjoy pleasure from it."]

6. Discouragements in Art.

Compare moderns with ancients. Consider the
latter, their care and culture of bodies themselves by
exercises, the Greek discipline. Wrestling, even of
the wrestlers in state (remember Pericles in Plutarch).
So a Scipio, when first Rome took the polite way. See
the passage of Livy when the commissioners from the
Senate were sent as inquisitors into his athletic and
other Greek manners.

Consider after the bodies and forms themselves,
the opportunity of viewing these forms of the finer
sort (not porters or beggars) in nudity, and in easy,
familiar, as well as strenuous exercising action. For
as in a hot country, so in quotidian baths. In private
families, wives, children. Whereas now none but
painters (as Albani) used to such views, and these

---

[1] Quintilian's *Institutiones Oratoriae*, Lib. IX, cap. 4, l. 116, cited by
Junius in *de pictura veterum*, p. 38.

constrained and awkward as being lucrative only, necessitous, mercenary, and a reproach and shame in the passive parties.

Also distortions by dress, unnatural bandages, ligatures : as cravats, garterings, women's bodice and contraction of waist, pressure of hips, swellings and unnatural disfigurations of necks, breasts, paps. Borings and lugging down of ears by jewels, (well that it is not nostrils as with the other barbarians), perukes, cravats.

Also props or stilts under the heel or hind part of the foot, relaxing the hinder tendon and muscles ; and extending, stretching unnaturally those of the fore part and instep, setting us young a tiptoe. So women's figures of feet and legs wholly destroyed in China by small shoes, till they are unable to stand. Our case even among the lower sort very near the same ; a degree or two only removed from the same barbarism.

Hence no modern figure (of the noble kind) now extant in the world, which can be seen standing natur-ally on the ground.

Idea therefore must be taken from nature and drawn ; instinct and what is innate ; or from the ancient trunks and broken remains.

What little help from Academy in this respect, viz. of nudity's, i.e. naked porters, or privately from diseased courtesans. Whereas those who know nature under-stand well what difference debauch soon makes in the youngest female, and how deflowering is soon de-flowering in this sense also : the *flos* instantly vanishing.

Statuary[1] the mother art to painting. In the first place on account of religion and civil government (as these stood among the ancients), the families, heroes, patricians, patriots, etc. as well as *penates*. ("He deserves his statue in gold!" Modern expressions which show the nature of the thing.) And in the next place on account of the profound learning, muscles,

[1] *Infra*, p. 127.

anatomy, physique, symmetry, (a statue viewed all round), simplicity, purity.

Remember also what pity: Raphael forced to paint walls[1]; cartoons for tapestry ; an underwork man for false work ; altar pieces as the priests commanded ; popes enjoined (witness the transfiguration-piece[2], called the first picture of the world) saints with lights about their heads: sometimes gold and silver! rare works in art[3]!

False[4] criticism another discouragement in art. Upstart affected critics: Why this? Why that? General topics which they think mighty ingenious as: lights whence ? How here and yet there ?—Answer: Flying clouds, a thunder storm covering one spot; sun shining the stronger and brighter on another. A reflection from the rocks unseen. Other objects out of the picture in the very place of the spectator, whence new various mixed tints[5] of which nothing appears,—but the effect in the picture itself.

Also that other pert question of these sprightly critics, viz. "How does that garment hang on ? " Answer: "It does not hang at all. 'Tis dropping. You catch sight only in an instant." So in running

---

[1] *Infra*, p. 148.

[2] This transfiguration-piece of Raphael would have made an excellent marble or piece of relief-work (and such Raphael always carried in head : those of the ancients in default of pictures having been his great school and lesson). But as it is, in the illusive art 'tis so far from that sweet persuasiveness and illusion (sweet as it is in other respects) that it not only breaks all rule of perspective, but everything of general order, position or collocation. The mountain a mole-hill, at most a mountebank's stage. Those figures below which should be seen by the upper parts (supposing the point of sight to be above the flat of the mountain as it must be for the sake of the lying figures there) are not at all in the air. Every figure a point of light by itself may be cut out of the cloth, or stuck on any other cloth, anywhere as well as where they are. No *one* principal, no subjection, subordination, unity or integrity: no piece: no whole. All disposition and order sacrificed in this transfiguration-work, as all colouring in the cartoons.

[3] Quere. Whether no instance of this in Raphael's? Where or what other master's besides. Answer....

[4] Of true criticism (of which an art must be found) see 'Soliloquy,' vol. I, p. 240. "For to all music there must be an ear proportionable. There must be an art of hearing found." So of seeing, etc.

[5] *Infra*, p. 147.

figures, in a horse full speed, in the gladiator Farnese.
Whoever saw either of these subjects precisely and
distinctly in any such attitude? So a man falling from
a precipice. An angel, mercury flying. Michael
Angelo's, natural attraction of his resurrection figures
upwards (ill represented in the print, a poor one). All
these instantaneous. All is invention (the first part of
painting), creation, divining, a sort of prophesying
and inspiration, the poetical ecstatic and rapture.
Things that were never seen; no nor that ever were:
yet feigned. Painter as poet, a second maker[1].

But without all this apology and defence. The
poem and fiction is answer sufficient: the hyperbole,
the invention, essential; the probable, plausible; the
poetic, truth. What else would be every line in epic
exaggerated continally beyond all possibility if narrowly
searched. And see most particularly (what is of infinite curiosity and of usefulest speculation to us in
the research of painting) the Homerical and Virgilian
description of the shields, where the figures at last
insensibly begin to stir and move and do what is
absurd and impossible to imagine. Yet this is right.

Sad to consider that the occasional rise of painting,
being chiefly from the popish priesthood, the improvement and culture of it (excepting the vicious part for
the cabinets of the grandees etc.) has turned wholly
on the nourishment and support of superstition (chiefly
too in ugly forms), and exaltation of that vile shrivelling
passion of beggarly modern devotion (as in Miscellanys, pp. 126–8, and Letter of Enthusiasm, pp. 35–36).
Witness the best picture in the world, Domenichino's
St Jerome.

Remember here (as prefatory) to anticipate the
nauseating, the puking, the delicate, tender-stomached,
squeamish reader (pseudo or counter critic), *delica-
tulus.* "Why all this?" And "can't one taste or
relish a picture without this ado?" (So in Miscellany,
the prosopopy, pp. 166, 278.) Thus kicking, spurning

[1] See Char-cks, vol. I, p. 207.

at the speculation, investigating, discussion of the *je
ne sais quoy.*

Euge tuum et belle : nam belle hoc excute totum,
Quid non intus habet ?[1]

["Your 'well done!' and your 'O fine!' for examine
this whole 'Opine.' What has it not within?"]
So the "I like," "you like," who can forbear? who
does forbear? Therefore. Have patience. Wait the
tale. Let me unfold etc.
Chief support of painting what?—X[t]!—Wretched
model[2]. Barbarian. No form, no grace of shoulders,
breast[3], no *démarche*, air, majesty, grandeur, a lean
uncomely proportion and species, a mere Jew or
Hebrew (originally an ugly scabby people) both shape
and physique, with half beard peaked, not one or the
other. Lank clinging hair, snivelling face, hypocritical
canting countenance and at best melancholy, mad
and enthusiastical in the common and lower way, not
so well as even the bacchanals and bacchantes[4].

But of this more when we come to speak of
Decorum[5]. And there add (in notes): The painters,
without any manner of necessity or prescription that
I know of, represent the husband of the blessed virgin
as a broken, blind, doating old man, at the very birth
of our Lord and Saviour; though highly probable

---

[1] Persius, *Satires*, I.
[2] Mem[d]. Here the general subject. viz. God the Father a broken,
wrapt up, nursed, old; consumptive look, haggard, with carcass, a dead
Christ held forth in winding sheet, a pigeon in bosom, and a lubberly,
hober-de-hoy or two of an angel (hermaphroditical forms, half-man, half-
woman, in petticoats and broad flopping wings) with a dozen or score
of peepers, raw, callow heads (like gaping birds out of a nest) stuck in
unnaturally between a pair of wings without a body, and called cherubs.
From hence (as taking ground from a high station), thunder and rant
(but comical still and in good humour) against common prayer-book-
cult, glass window etc., tapestry figures of high church and chapel.
Better the perfect in the kind ; and statuary introduced. Altar a true
altar, and image etc. as becoming. And justify this by Queen Elizabeth's
rant cited by an ingenious author and learned gentleman (M'C——). Is
priestcraft in perfection. (Cite the cited authority but not M'C., nor his
pamphlet by name.)
[3] Here cite the poets, finest works of Apollo, Jove.
[4] Of which see below, p. 126.   [5] *Infra*, p. 167.

(and better to be supported) that according to the
Jewish practice, highly commendable in suitable
marriages and regard, veneration, that the parties were
of equal or suitable age. And now thirty and odd
years after, the same Joseph is seen going out without
kindred in search of Christ.

7. ENCOURAGEMENTS, MOTIVES.

1. Invention of prints, etchings (which are
original) answerable to printing in the commonwealth
of letters. Hence eye of the public framed; though
injured by the false (French and Flemish) taste, and
ill cuts in books of learning: always ill because of
cheapness of the impression.
2. As to the benefit to mankind and the youth:
not only *emollit mores*[1], but forms. Diverts the noble
(and idle) from extravagant expense of time and
estate: gaming: riot: excess: lazy habit and its
consequences[2].
3. Πολλάκις ἐθαύμασα... and upon that tone to
remark, observe, " How great an ambition in nobility,
gentry, wits, etc., to be knowing in master's hands."
Comparisons drawn from painting, poets, orators,
divines. Lives of painters, even modern and mere
wretches such as they are, much canvassed, emphatically related, in the best companys, among ladies, etc.[3]
Also this concerning excursions, deviations, diverting tales, episodes, miscellany, occasional reflections
(partly as Lucullus said, for my own sake). I have
always thought strange that authors should be found
(and readers to support them) who could purpose,
write, and couch their fragments and spare thoughts,
as if pity the world should lose the least[4].

---

1 [Ovid, *Epistola ex Ponto*, Lib. II, Epist. 9, l. 48.]
2 As below, p. 174.
3 This in the preface and introductory part, with much thrown off into
notes below it. See also about the master painters' lives and occasional
relation of their personal and hand characters, resembling and instructive
as well as entertaining. See I say above, p. 15.
4 See ' Soliloquy,' p. 164, and ' Miscellanys,' pp. 145—6.

With respect to self, (apologizing for it). Thus reconciliation of plastics, etc., viz. That being sick and under pains, watches, insomnias, etc., as also disturbing business or affairs overmuch for one in a low habit, etc. The custom of viewing the forms and raising these pleasing spectres, not only good as chasers, drivers away of other species and haunting forms of faces, grimaces, etc., in weak stomachs, indigestions, head aches ; but in reality helping the passions, calming, allaying, introducing new. But this conditionally, that the just virtuoso-rules be practised, and none of the frightful or ghastly spectacles (as Apollo, executioner of martyrs, in the very flaying act), any more than the lascivious be admitted. For each of these are false and never ryparography.

8.   PRAISES, RECOMMENDATIONS OF THE ART.

Had I been born a Christian Catholic where Christianity and imagery was natural cult, etc., I should say to myself, or as I now am, shall say to such a one, in favour of poor art and artists, recognized however by heaven and divine law (*jure divino*) : " Sir! Can you worship thus ? Would doggerel serve you for hymns ? bagpipe or jews' harp for music and hallelujahs ? Can you see Christ twice crucified ? Him broken and distorted of whom it was said *a bone of him*, etc. ? Him disfigured of whom it is written... ? Him decrepit, gouty, old, etc., who never had a blemish, wound, or disease ; and who was so young a man still when he suffered ? Him who was purposely by the wicked placed between two thiefs in disgrace, made resembling to such countenances, and of the same looks, mien, form and passion as either rascal ? "
Dilemma about the use of pictures by Christians. Either none or good. Church of England, (High Church) and Lutheran miserable. And in this sense *odi imitatores* as in ' Characteristics.'

And here again in favour of painters: To insist[1]
that beautiful forms beautify; polite, polish. On the
contrary, gothic gothicize, barbarous barbarize.
In respect of economy and as delivering from
other luxuries and expences when rightly taken. First
because of its own nature; τὸ καλόν; expensiveness
and richness being the very ruin of the art according
to Pliny in the 'Characteristics.'
Also for reasons hinted just below[2]. And here a
place for moralizing. "Everyone covets in proportion
to the appetite of expence: not florid and generous as
is vulgarly conceived, but modest and generous. Love
of giving, largition, communication, joined with hatred
of waste and needless expence.—Frugal *ergo* liberal.—
Saving *ergo* bountiful." A good father, excellent man
I knew, taught his lad to fling away farthings in view
of generosity. This directly the contrary road and I
fear would sooner teach him avarice, increasing his
wants by negligence, and his appetites not decreasing.
On the contrary his ill appetites and affections rising
stronger by the contempt of other peoples wants and
the noble pleasure of relieving them by what he neglects
and spurns. Hence heart hardened.
The Roman *vir frugi*. The first Cato. Above
all the Englishman, because of a court and place-pre-
ferment, prostitution, etc.
But in a way it may be objected: "That this
makes against our subject, viz. Pictures." If it does
so, so let it. Let it take its chance. God's name.
But let us see first. Examine the true taste, etc.
In some of the early divisions[3] (whether the beginning or middle of part or chapter) raise the objection
of luxury and expence encouraged in the great, and
consequently too in the little according to Esop's and
Horace's Frogs so unto themselves. But first a compromise, a compounding, a less for a greater and
worse; a taking off from play, equipage, riot and feast.

[1] *Supra*, p. 104.   [2] *Infra*, p. 123.
[3] *Supra*, p. 123.

Nay even from building; and in the next place when
the extravagance is committed and the *res*, the patrimony hurt (of which speak seriously as the way to
knavery, etc., in the gentleman).   All may be retrieved
and upon a new turn of business with a good air disposed of, and with good advantage and increase of the
principal, if such rules as these are followed and not fancy.

For this is worthy observation that though we
scarce see a man whose fancy agrees with another in
the many hands and paintings, yet in general when
the cabal[1] is over, for this must be excepted (as in
Poussin's case in France and Domenichino's in Naples),
the public always judges right, and the pieces esteemed
or disesteemed after a time and a course of some years
are always exactly esteemed according to their proportion of worth by these rules and studies.   So that
the gentleman who follows his caprice may undo
himself.   But he who either fixes his taste, or buys
according to the universal judgment and public taste
and confession of painters in works of the deceased,
will never be abused or come off a sufferer when he
parts with his effects.

Also secret apology (in passing and not with set
design) for purchasing of pictures: because of necessity
of purchasing as a virtuoso for commerce and acquaint-
ance in Italy.   This to be thrown in in raillery and
humour upon my Lord ... etc., and addressing to him
as the cause of drawing me in.   And there being a
necessity withal of speaking of self (another kind of
self-citation) because of these purchases[2].

9.   ANCIENT MASTERS AND WORKS, IN STATUES, HEADS, RELIEFS, INTAGLIOS.

Beginning of ancient reform, improvement and
perfection of iconics, plastics, and graphical imitation,

[1] In notes refer to Fréart and Bosse about this Cabal against Poussin.
Supra, p. 15; *infra*, p. 128.
[2] See above, p. 98.

about the same time with the poetical (after the great model Homer) in the two branches of dramatic, viz. tragedy and comedy.

Euripides before and Menander just after Apelles and Protegenes; or near upon their contemporaries. The art of colours being not in its perfection (or beyond four) till then.

Therefore statuary[1] first in order of time (history and nature: as said of other arts in Char-cks). Then painting. For *design* indeed the foundation: colours an after ornament (and to be regarded by tyros), though drawing perfect of necessity when statuary perfect. Therefore Leukis not yet an Apelles. And had Raphael ever had an equal since him in idea and grace, he had been surpassed and not the first and only great in painting, because of some improvement perhaps in colouring after, tho—.

Egyptians though so much earlier and so vastly ancient; yet barbarous. Why? A law in this case. Orthodox designing, hieroglyphics[2], sacred-monstrous, reformation of these first forms, sacrilegious, heretical. National church-painting. Figures of the gods still monstrous (though somewhat Greek) whilst in Asia or Africa: as Jupiter, Hammon, Diana of Ephesus, Anubis, Canopus....

The animals once ill designed as at first when given by Isis, or other sovereigns to be kept alive and mourned for when happening to die (being in memory of mangled husband whose true body was still concealed[3]).

These animal forms, I say, being never after to be innovated.

The religion of the Egyptians being thus made *specific*[4], both internally within themselves and with

[1] *Supra*, p. 117.   [2] *Supra*, p. 92.
[3] See Herodotus, Diodorus Siculus.
[4] So the Jewish religion *specific*. Christian not till after Christ and settled by successional authority. E.g. had a proselyte to the Jewish temple and religion been at Jerusalem, or in Judea at the preaching of Christ and been converted, afterwards carried away and lost in a foreign

still greater division and abhorrence from externs. Not thus the Greek, Roman, and other heathen worthies. For here an emperour, or philosopher, or historian (as Herodotus) travelling, could be initiated severally in each worship.

Note that all the true antique figures, and especially the single female[1] heads or busts of bacchanals, have a deep, eager, severe ecstatic or enthusiastic air. Nothing like disorder from wine: nothing drowsy, frolicsome, wanton, or so much as gay or smiling; but on the contrary stern and rigid, the passion of the plain, prophetic, oraculous kind, fanatic and lymphatic (as in Letter of Enthusiasm, etc.). Whence the guess[2] of Heinsius, (though so rash an obtruder) wonderfully engaging and persuasive, entering into the spirit of the Ode of Horace there cited[3] and into the rest of antiquity as by these figures and heads of bacchanals, is so confirmed and illustrated. Also the place in Livy, *ibid.* (viz. Letter of Enthusiasm, p. 47) and Miscellanys, pp. 39, 40, 66, 67 and notes. Full of the Holy Ghost.—Full of grace (as the Molinists and Quietists, mystics, quakers, new prophets). Same passion by modern painters in some of their saints[4].

Against Academy life-painting (as inferiour to study

land like China or Japan: in this case he would not have been a specific, unless he had an apostolic revelation or mission, but at liberty to have relinquished the Jews even though he found a synagogue, circumcision, and sabattizing in that very new country to which he was carried. Thus also during the controversy between Paul and Peter, the Christian religion less specific: whilst one conformed the other absolutely dissented from the Jewish rites with anger and reflection on the occasional-conformist Peter. And thus also the Protestant sects more or less specific, as they allow latitude and communion with others: not absolutely damning, condemning. But the Church of Rome absolutely specific, as exclusive, peremptory, negatively and affirmatively.

This by way of explanation only of the phrase *specific.* So to return again to our *specific forms,* the barbarous sculpture and hieroglyphic notes of the Aegyptian priests.

[1] See Leonardo Agostini's *Le Gemme Antiche,* partie 1ᵉ, Fig. 27, pp. 28 and so to 34 inclusive.

[2] Viz. *Lymphatur* for *Lactatur.* For no joy in the case. "I have seen God. I shall die." See Scripture.

[3] Letter of Enthusiasm, p. 51.

[4] As for instance see in modern masters, *infra,* p. 127.

of ancient forms and culture of ideas). Let but anyone read Plutarch and Xenophon on the Spartan
discipline, diet, and care of breed, conception, birth
and nurture of bodies, and then wonder, if he can, why
ancient life beyond modern (porters), and Spartans
beyond even the rest of the Greeks in number of
victories at the Olympics; or that Leonidas and his
six hundred at Thermopylae, etc.

(1) Ancient masters how much honoured and in
repute from Xeuxis and Apelles, Fabius Pictor, etc.
to Diognetus, Marcus's master....

(2) Philosophy itself out of the school of design
and plastic art. Sophroniscus's son of whose own hand
the graces, etc.

(3) In the question, whether the statuary or painter
—the noblest. Remember, that besides Socrates, of
Sophroniscus, etc. and his graces. Nothing mechanical
and even much less than painting, though seemingly
the contrary. For note the story of Raphael contend-
ing with Michael Angelo, and making (by command
and precept to an ordinary stone-carver) one of the
perfectest, if not the perfectest, of modern statues.
Also the ancient statuarys wrought more immediately
for the temples, the *lares*, the gods, heroes, patriots,
ancestors, magistrates, etc. The painters more for
pleasure and beauteous contemplation.

(4) Here statuary the mother art of painting[1].

10. MODERN MASTERS AND WORKS, IN PAINTING, ETCHING, ETC.

What our English life-writer says of the enthusiasm
of Domenichino.

Enthusiasm represented by modern masters, when
of the prophetic ecstatic kind—as by ancient masters[2]
—in the persons of St Paul, the prophet Jeremiah,
Saul.

---

[1] *Supra*, p. 117.   [2] *Supra*, p. 126.

Monsieur du Fresnoy[1], who wrote the *Ars Graphica*, was himself a painter, according to our English translator[2]. Quere. What for a performer?—This highly material because of his being an author.

Quere also (for the same reason) about Leonardo da Vinci[3], so extolled by the French author Fréart, who was refuted on this point; it having been shown that this piece (which he brags of having translated) was not of Leonardo da Vinci, nor of any worth; as the excellent Poussin testifies in his letter, if it be genuine and undoubted as published by Monsieur Bosse in his *Peintre*[4].

Censure of Annibale Carracci[5]. His noted piece frequently engraved, etched by Carlo Marat with great exactness (viz. Christ and Samaritan Woman). Action all theatrical[6]. Imitation of an imitation; at second hand; not immediate, not original, from nature. Art by custom becomes a new model.

So the tragic, or the stage. Each nation (as French and English, *vice versa*) finds this better in their contrary than in themselves. Mon[r] Baron. Our M[rs] Barry. So the dancing-master[7] if strictly followed: a fictitious,

---

[1] *Infra*, p. 140.

[2] Anonymous publisher who praises him. [Cf. C. du Fresnoy's *The Art of Painting*, translated by M. Dryden. Lond. 1750.]

[3] A Florentine great mathematician, anatomist, and older than Raphael. Rival of, in art, and restorer of modern painting, according to our English author (in Dryden's Fresnoy, p. 278).

[4] p. 56.

[5] Mem[d]. Speak of his gallery with just applause, that being after his contemplation of the ancient forms and study of Raphael, for which I have heard him censured by the best modern heads of eminent painters and virtuosi: "Forsooth! as varying from his finer early manner and delicacy of his great predecessor, leader, and countryman Correggio, from whence his Lombard school."

[6] Theatrical, etc. (see "Notion of Hercules," chap. III, 7), or, which is the same as theatrical action, pulpit-action, as in foreign catholic-country. (This may be safely pushed to ridicule, our own priests accompanying the laugh; though against their real interest and art at the bottom.) And from hence I have known a real able, but devout painter fall in raptures on the pathetic action of the Christ, the touch of the single finger on the breast (the other fingers in apt position about), when by this he really and truly showed and even demonstrated to me, the affectation I suspected, and which I was always willing in honour of Carracci to pass by uncriticised. [7] *Supra*, p. 110.

false and affected gesture and mien: not the natural bow, tread or entrance into a room.

The painter more than the poet should beware of this (though even in tragedy Horace says: *Et tragicus plerumque dolet sermone pedestri*[1]) ["So tragical generally, in their pain take to the language of prose"] by reason that...

Modern masters no learning. No converse till after raised and known by their pencil, and then too late. Illiberal. Dis-ingenuous. Sharks, rakes. What ideas, when thus vulgar! Not even so high as what we call good breeding and manners in a common sense. What sense of poetic manners, characters, personages, moral truth! What kind of judges! Yet these give the clue and lead the great, who are cheated as well as misled by these mechanic knaves.

History of revival of painting. How far owing to Roman hierarchy[2] (see Char-cks, vol. III, p. 90). But liberty withal, viz. the hierarchy itself (archon for life, ephori, generals of orders, jesuits etc.), and also civil liberty, the free states of Italy as Venice, Genoa, and then Florence also and other places. Besides that, meeting and as it were co-habiting as private men, but grandees, in one city (as in Rome, or at a carnival in Venice). This reduces things to a parity with a free state and independency which sets painters and artists free, erects a public, a nation, Italy (see Machiavelli's passion for Italy as the Greek φιλέλληνα), excites emulation etc., creates a taste, judgment.

[1] *De Arte Poetica*, l. 95.
[2] Mem[d]. Under this head of the hierarchy remark in notes, viz. "That we in particular (viz. Anglo-saxons) and church (*quatenus* Christian, independent of the magistracy and act of parliament) are but a colony of the papal hierarchy from Pope Gregory and his missionary monk," etc. (as in Characteristics, vol. III, p. 239, and N.B.). That notwithstanding the Pope's great enmity to letters (true letters: though himself so rhetorical) yet what care of music and magnificence! See in his life, in Platina and Monsieur Bayle. Glad would he have been after extirpation of ancient heathen beauties (a reproach as he thought) to have revived art, statuary, idols, etc., upon the finest model and taste, provided it had been new and like the attempted new christian poem (page 240 of the same third volume of the Char-cks) on the foundation of Christ, etc.

Story of Domenichino (here in Naples, *ergo*) from
Signor Paulo, after I had been to see the chapel of
the town-saint (St Janͬ), called the treasury in the
archiepiscopal great church. Whereupon a consul-
tation held by the ――― convoked. Poor Domenichino
was rated by the head : they wisely supposing that he
would make no bodies without heads, and therefore
concluding that a head must carry a body at ten crowns[1]
per head. So the poor painter stuck the vaults with
heads (cherubim and seraphim) as an orange with
cloves to get his bread : the hard even at this rate.
The work therefore unfinished, unstudied, and much
of it unworthy of him. The pretty *peepers* still very
amiable and executable even by their gentility and
prettiness. But sometimes even a bishop and principal
figure peeps, which is very unsuitable ; and sometimes
such a figure stretched out too far in length, a mere
whole profile because easier studied and as it were
taking breath, or making way for thicker heads to
appear the more excusably in clusters elsewhere.

How judge of such things without knowledge of
these facts and lives of the painters themselves.

Poussin wonderful, when considered according to
paragraph (3) of the Notion ; and chiefly when considered also as a *Frenchman*! and working in little[2].

Apply to Poussin's character what stands in Char-
cks[3], viz. fidelity to art. This plainly the cause of
his discontent in France and being set and over-
powered by the cabal. This the reason why he afterwards[4] naturalized himself a Roman : resolved not to
betray his art or renounce his manner. Drawing in
little (of which the very kind is in strictness without
truth) was the utmost he would do. But his other
work of figures tolerably sizeable.

---

[1] Ducats, viz. five to our pound.
[2] Hint withal his learning and education as in English lives (Du
Fresnoy's *Art of Painting*, tr. p. 359), with reproach on other painters as
illiterate.
[3] Vol. I, p. 261.
[4] See if this be sure.

Reason for this little manner, viz. cabinet-furniture, *pieces-de-cabinet* for ladies and the court. Ladies hate the great manner; love baby-sizes, toys, miniature. Besides this the churches and palaces (that are spacious) were filled ere this by the multitude of tolerable good pieces, since the Carracci's school. And therefore according to our love of novelty and the humour of the age he found this to be the most enabling him to get a living by a moderate price (such as he set upon his pieces with great integrity), the roof, staircase, cupola, and fresco-painting (the chief in vogue) being abhorrent from his chaste, severe, just and accurate genius, which therefore kept itself to tablature and home-study, wisdom, nature, philosophy, history, criticism, learning.

11. PAINTERS :—CHARACTER, EDUCATION, QUALIFICATION[1].

The face painter, limner (as Cooper, Sir Godfrey Kneller, Riley etc.), no study of their works after the knack and colouring got. No workmanship, no labour, no not so much as thought, but when the party is sitting and sees. The patron lord or lady sees and is witness to all the industry, pains, or study, there is in the business : nothing when their back is turned. But when a subject is given to a real painter, a heroic great subject: Good heavens! What toil! What study! What meditation requisite! The five parts resolved, accommodated, determined. 1st. *Invention* raised. 2d. *Forms* passed in review, proportion chosen suitably. 3d. *Colouring* and *tints* in the same manner suitable: if tragical, tragic, and so in general and particular each figure with harmony considered. 4th. The *passions*, moral, thought, sentiment, manners. —What a study. And 5th, the *collocation*, general symmetry, disposition, as a general making his disposition and order of battle when about to engage.

---

[1] See Junius' passages on this head.

9—2

What restless nights! What brown studies, reveries,
ecstatic veins, *rabiosa silentia* etc.!

Here remember what said of Michael Angelo.
Domenichino...when surprised, overheard, or spied
through a key-hole or chink, in agitation, trembling,
rolling on the ground, on all fours, prancing, caprioling
(like a horse or quadruped monster when such a one
was to be imagined, designed), gaping, staring, mur-
muring, roaring. So my painter (Closterman) going
into his picture when in the dark and standing long
before it.

How great a shame for such an artist as a "painter
(an epic, heroic-one) to know less of mathematics,
measuring, statics, common principles, or rules of
mechanic art, than the most ordinary mechanic, the
house carpenter, common surveyor, head bricklayer,
or inferiour architect! For the statuary, his very
measuring tools and plumets will set him in the way!"

Michael Angelo[1] to be justified against the French
and other bigot attacks. Pietro Belloris denial of
Vasaris and the received account of his having taught
Raphael; and particularly against the French author,
Fréart de Chambray[2]. Whose as impertinent censure of
Raphael (his pretended favourite and abominably wrong
commended, as if it were praising Both[3] upon his
Judgment of Paris) in his Massacre of the Innocents[4].

Jordano. Rabble painter, not only as painting
rabble best (witness his rout of Holofernes' camp in
the treasury roof of the Carthusians at Naples, and
his great door piece at the entrance of the church of
St Girolimi, *ibid.*); but as disguising himself best in

---

[1] Confer with Sensus Communis, p. 144 note. And below, p. 154.
Mon[r] Fréart (according to his dogmatical character) reasons only on a
wretched print: having never seen the original; or if he had, having
no eye in painting; only a good thought and maxim from affection to
the ancients, and Raphael their student.

[2] Fréart de Chambray, *An idea of the perfection of painting*, translated
by J. Evelyn. Lond. 1668, pp. 14, 64, 70.

[3] [The text refers probably to Jan Both's painting in the National
Gallery (no. 209) in which the figures are by Poelenburgh.]

[4] See his pages 47, 48 and *supra*, p. 16.

PLASTIC ART

133

a multitude, in a confusion, heap, variety of tints, and mad figures, especially the imperfect ones at a distance do wonders. See what is applied of the chorus singers[1] (like the French). Can't sing alone, or with a *il corbo*, or few strings accompanying.

Spaniolet[2]: Bust painter, half figures, and of old ugly figures, fierce style (from M. Ang. de Caravaggio), no drawing, the antipode of grace (witness his rival picture to Domenichino, in the treasury of the great church), horrid, monstrous, is said to be well from waist upward, an executioner, from whence below. And indeed all his whole[3] figures, like himself barbarous and horrid.

12. Subjects of Painting.

Through indulgence to the fashionable taste (viz. gallantry and amours, as in tragedy and poem, so in epic tablature) give for a subject and pattern of the *ultima linea* in this kind: 'The History of Bacchus and Ariadne.'

Firstly. Both sexes in perfect beauty; as heroic then machine : (Juno, whom as Pronuba I would prefer to Venus, cupids being allowed in a distinct group in the air or otherwise, so as not to intermix with Juno, or her car, or attendance). And in the next place as to the camps or perspective, both land and sea (Ariadne having been left on an island) with the beauties of both as far as the principal life will allow, and thus grove, rock, port and shipping, a descent and train. A kind of oration, solemn march, or triumph. The hero and chief in agriculture and benefaction to mankind, a conqueror with benignity, in opposition to a ravager, a mars, a nimrod. Thirdly. The form perfect. Age, youth, strength, no decay, no rawness, much less fat, or bloating (as illiterate artists of the moderns represent), but rather over-slim

[1] *Infra*, p. 176.   [2] [Spagnoletto] *supra*, p. 15.
[3] *Supra*, p. 15.

and effeminate, like the Eastern princes, whence he came conqueror with the softness of their manners; not those of the Northern Thrace, who abused his gift and were thence noted for quarrels—Pugnare, Thracum est[1]. Fourthly. Ariadne's form, the same with chastity waiting him in the marriage bower (as in Xenophon who chose this subject for his Symposium); yet being widow not virgin may be allowed better to wait him with secret but modest joy, intermixt with sorrow because of her abandoned state. Sixthly. The comic part (as in Homer himself) viz. satires, fawns, etc. in the train and dance after Bacchus.

13. SORTS OF PAINTERS AND PAINTING: PORTRAITURE, RYPAROGRAPHY, GROTESQUE, BATTLE PAINTING, ETC.

Portraiture. Face painting being almost the whole of portraiture (as profiles and mere busts in medals and the like). The artist may be and almost ever is ignorant of anatomy, proportions, and the five parts, excepting a small matter of the outline (enough for copying, since a copy after a face or a figure taken in a cloth is much the same) together with some part or degree of the third part, viz. colouring. And with this he may set up for a painter and great in his way, with drapery's, etc.; if perhaps, he hires not another as is usual to do this, or anything that happens if beyond a mere common figure singly or a single head. Thus good face painters and medalists, etc. without further study. For if perhaps a genius, capable; it must be checked and spoilt: witness Van Dyck[2], Sir

[1] Horace, *Ode* xxvii, l. 2.
[2] A portrait painter (as Van Dyck) attempts a family piece, puts figures together in an action, lays a scene, unites, makes a disposition, etc. But this is launching out of his depth. Better a history painter if strongly invited should descend to this work for some great and understanding patron or Prince—for if not understanding cannot be satisfied with the work on account of subordination, and 2^d, 3^d and 4th figures disobliged—than that the accustomed face-painter should offer to ascend so high as this, in which he will prove an Icarus. For so Van Dyck: fantastic, apish, antic in his action, and wretched and false in his composition, collocation, etc.

P. Lilly. And thus our Cooper, Peter Oliver, and others in miniature, were perfect in face painting, ignorant in design and art, mere mechanics. This not so much as a liberal art nor to be so esteemed; as requiring no liberal knowledge, genius, education, converse, manners, moral-science, mathematics, optics, but merely practical and vulgar. Therefore not deserving honour, gentility, knighthood conferred[1].

Even an indifferent person[2], who neither in mien nor habit carries any similitude to any known species, rank, or class (as neither senator, or judge, soldier, scholar, or philosopher, saint, monk[3], or priest, good fellow, rake, squander, wild youth, enamorata, courtier, cook[4], country-squire, etc.), yet being known particularly, and very remarkable, citable, much talked of, much praised, much ridiculed, or bantered by his club, cabal, set of friends, or known in such and such walks, such coffee-house, in the side-box, at St James or Hyde Park, Mr Such-a-one, Mr What-do-you-call-him, Mr Thing-um. This personage, this very phiz (as they say) is for the time that he is known and remembered, and whilst the human lasts a pleasing imitation, and makes the artist by chance and unknowingly "a poet-painter for the time being." Even this a *character*[5], and the work *characteristical* instructs[6]. ("How like! Just he for all the world!") But the humour over once, the jest spent; and where is the sense, the thought? The piece sinks again into its nothing. Its no character. It dies and becomes

---

[1] Glance at Sir Kneller. Am not reflecting on King W^m: yet see again, *infra*, note 3.   [2] *Supra*, p. 102.

[3] Monk : Remember Van Dyck's friar, which old Lord Bradford had of Closterman. An imitation of an imitation (of a hypocrite, not really mortified, but how refined! how artful and near nature in the original, viz. the actor, the priest himself!). A fiction after a fiction, yet even thus *characteristical*, a *character*: with his death head and seeming mortified face. Not so on the stage. See Dryden's Spanish friar and Sir G. Kneller after Lee. Even this characteristical, and though reiterate still pleasing.

[4] A cook. And so down through all the order of ryparography, as below, p. 136.   [5] See above in Characters, p. 99.

[6] Sic oculos, sic ille manus, sic ora ferebat. Aeneid, lib. 3.

thoughtless, void of meaning; and all the art in the world
is thrown away. 'Tis an abuse of real art which should
(aye and will) be reserved for better purpose. For if
the painter deigns to hold to this work, his art and
genius will not deign to attend him thus employed.
He may excel in this, but (as Van Dyck) sacrifice his
ability in all else.

This remark as to the epic artist when he becomes
face painter, or worker in portraiture, viz. "That
besides the subjecting of his genius, narrowing of his
thought, contraction of his idea, deadening of his fancy,
constraining of his hand, disaccustomed him in the
freedom of his pencil, tying him down to copying, trans-
lating, servilely submitting to the lords and ladies, etc.,
his originals. Besides all that, I say he looks his time
and fame. These works buried: those immortal;
these scarce one in twenty worth purchasing by a
stranger: those the same to all people and all nations.
And as he proceeds, he improves. He gains not only
in his experience, but by the spreading of his works
abroad, which spread his name, bring custom to him
while living, honours both while living and (what is
the generous artist's great spur as it is the hero's) after
life, both in his own country and foreign nations."

Ryparography. Ryparography though by itself
naught, yet to be understood and used by the heroic
masters to mix (but much modified) with his *heroic*
as the foil. So often Raphael himself; a cook, a
pharisee, a thyrsites, amidst the other homerical forms.

The prince of critics and great judge of arts dis-
tinguishes painters into the *heroic*, who paint them
better than the common life, better than they are
by nature; the *ridiculous*, lower *comic*, who paint them
worse than the common life, worse than they naturally
are; and a *middle sort*, who paint them true and just
as they are. But then this truth in heroic is falsehood,
and a blur against the truth of art and the hypothesis
itself; whether it be Scripture and history which is
posed or laid down, or whether heathen gods or

heroes, or even great men, Roman and Grecian chiefs, consecrated as it were by age, time, and history.

In the middle kind, when according to truth, may be comprehended fairs, camps, public places in modern cities, hunting matches, and parties of pleasure, of gentlemen and ladies, (where the figures, not the perspective *paysage* or animals are principal)...

In the last detestable and odious kind, excels the Flemish...Brouwer, ῥὒπᾰρογράφοι.

Grotesque. All grotesque painting not ryparography; though most may be such. Witness Raphael's monsters and grotesque after the ancients, in Sign^r Bartoli's book of prints, etc.

Remember also to acknowledge the excellence and attainment of perfection in the vulgar life and abject[1] base life by modern masters. But not so as to the heroic, epic, lyric (not even Raphael entirely; for how clogged! how diverted! how prostituted!). Only the doggerel, farce, burlesque. Parody: first comedy: satire: mimes. But not tragedy: latter not comedy, not after an iliad like the verses given to —— on which he formed his olympic Jove.

Battle Painting. Battle painting though modern and little; yet next joined to humanity (proportionately little) because of the horse noble animal, and next to man. Of the horse treat elsewhere, remembering the noble cast of the eye and head; the sublime air; the triton horses; the hero horses, half or quarter deities such as Achilles' Xanthus and his speech (a noble subject for painting!), on which mention Homer and the Père Bossu's excuse by Balaam's ass. The enthusiasm and inspiration expressible in the heathen subject and poet, not in the sacred one, not to be attempted (I fear) with any success. This historically true: poetically false. In the other (with the religious heathen, who could join both) what effect[2]!

---

[1] By masters Flemish, not worthy of being mentioned. The boorpainters.
[2] See Letter of Enthusiasm, pp. 4, 5, 6, 7.

Battle painting if in little figures (unfinished and therefore true as said just before) is to be esteemed but as a species of perspective, (according to what is said in Notion, chap. v, par. 10). The same as to buildings and architecture, if the perspective painter's genius leads to architecture. But if the architecture be so far principal and eminent as to drown, or as it were devour the field, and stand single by itself without a town, people and natural appurtenances of a town-prospect; or without a country, ruins, rocks, wood and natural appurtenances of a rural or country prospect: in this case the species of painting is empty, foolish, false, and below still life. For this at least is true and taking in vases, and other proportionable and artful pieces; and contains as well the rules of mathematics, or mathematical mechanics, and elegant workmanship.

Ship Painting. Ship painting (whether storms or calms), in which the Dutch, as they well may, excel, is also no more than a species of perspective; the rest being the mere knowledge of a hulk and ropes (no extraordinary science, not above the ship-wrights); but if joined with rock, sky, sea-port, etc.: then *right* and a *true* though inferiour species of perspective.

Miniature or Limning. "Miniature (viz. the diminutive kind) if finished is false; if unfinished and true serves only as machine work, appendix, or ornament to perspective."

Exception in this place for small portraiture of heads only (for bodies would be mere puppets and ridiculous as everyone presently sees), which convenience and use renders agreeable and friendship amiable. So enamel and water colours (viz. in miniature still. For even roof-work and fresco is water-coloured and so Raphael's cartoons though bigger than life). But enamel especially being generally little and in its nature glossy is still more false; though the ancients who had not our way in oil had another (as they had many now lost) of burning, which way for the largest as well as least manner, and what was highly esteemed, as by Pliny's remark of the master's inscriptions of their names ἐνέκαον.

Exception also in general for miniature or the diminutive kind in statuary[1], sculpture, etc., and for all works in the plastic kind, or of one substance, or even on a superiour plane with lines as lapidary or medal-imitations, or draughts in two colours, claro-oscuro, etc. on account of reason given in Notion[2].

Besides that there is no perspective field, or accompanying nature (sky, ground, distances, appendices, etc.). And for high or low relief, the medal-learning and antiquary science of anaglyphics (so necessary in society and for the use of mankind), as also the mere use and currency of coinage and money (another necessity) familiarizes and executes this diminutive manner in other kinds, which are not fully, supremely and strictly imitative painting.

Remember the reverse of the common phrase (speaking of meadows and perspective). "'Tis as if it were painted."—Ridiculous!—Therefore this is just what should not be painted. And therefore when a real good picture is to be commended say of it: "This is like perfect nature and not like paint." For when *nature* herself paints (as sometimes in wantonness and as it were luxuriantly) she ought not to be imitated: not the picture, but *herself* only (her pure *self*) copied.

Concerning mixture of works, master with master (as "perspective by such a one, figures by such a one or such a one") wholly false. So in my Claude de Lorrain, figures by Jordano, the latter giants and out of size, though moderately in harmony as to colouring. Remember Montague House, which I was never willing to go to see after rebuilt and painted, because the better the masters the more violent the conflict

---

[1] And thus of old certain considerable statuary commended in the little way as.... See Pliny.

But of painters above that I remember...Search for these in Pausanias, Pliny, Philostratus.

[2] Chap. v, p. 12.

and dissonance harsher. For though a man may submit to *himself* in this regard (though even the judicious Poussin—that equally great master in both kinds—sometimes failed in this and could not be enough below himself in perspective pieces), yet never to *another*. But Gaspar his brother-in-law (by him taught) and being able only in the perspective part, was through necessity perhaps (though with judgment joined) a perfect model of truth of this kind[1].

14. THE FIVE PARTS IN PAINTING.
General Considerations.

Monsieur Du Fresnoy's *Ars Graphica*[2]: whether worthy of notice?

1. If worthy note that the five parts of painting are wrongly reduced to three, by the marginal notes added, contrary to the sense of the author; who is not distinct in the five parts, has however reckoned four at least, and would have made no such enumeration as three according to the text.

2. In the first place, in the article of satire, or way of anticipation by raillery, censure, etc. (as necessary according to miscellaneous style to turn off ridicule, excite the nauseating palate by piquancy and feed the fashionable spleen). Remember to note the wrong impertinent blundering application of the plastic rules.

Scarce at any time in any of our modern poets or authors one single metaphor, allusion, allegory, simile grounded on the art and formed on the painter's business, but what makes the painter blush, the artist lose himself, not cognizable in the description or comparison. Something silly, preposterous and betraying ignorance.

---

[1] Expose in this place the civil war, riot, hub-bub, sedition, tumult, uproar of pieces, parts, colours, etc. in mixed works. Cupola of the Treasury at Naples, the Jesuits, *ibid.* And refer reciprocally to Notion, chap. v, par. 2 and 9.

[2] [Cf. C. A. Du Fresnoy's *The Art of Painting*, translated by Mr Dryden, Lond. 1750.]

3. Also comparisons and parallel ran between painting and poetry because of the *pictoribus atque poetis*[1] [painters and poets] etc. and the *ut pictura poesis*[2] [poems are as paintings] almost ever absurd and at best constrained, lame, or defective.

One says....Another says....

As to habits, dresses and all which painters comprehend in the common phrase of *drapery* should it be asked: " In which of the five parts do we place this?" 'Tis answered: " In the first and third." For not only invention, but history and learning lie in the first part. And for whatever in art goes further than the outline, must in respect of the draperies, be wholly in the third part (viz. light and shadow and colouring). There being properly no symmetry or regular mensuration of mere foldings so as to require anything of the second part; and much less life or passion, so as to have to do at all in the fourth. And as for the fifth, the general collocation, it is either included or carried along with the figures and bodies which it adorns, or it comes in like architecture, or trees, as making part of the masses or balancing parts in the perspective; and as such, it belongs indirectly and not immediately to part second.

1st Part in Painting: Invention. Story. Imagery.

This being the first of the (five) parts in painting; though in poetry 'tis the Σύνεσις, collocation, whole, unity, as the French author (Mon[r] Fréart de Chambray) has made it also in painting: but not with parity of reason. Since the manner of signature, designation, or image making is common to the poet with the rest of mankind, especially the literate, viz. by words, written characters of speech, grammar, etc.

But the painter's or plastic's manner, means, or medium peculiar to himself and art; not common to him with others. A man complete in wit, science, letters, politeness and even in the very judgment[1] of design : yet no *designer*, no hand, nor idea in order to a hand.

Therefore in this first part is involved the *materia plastica*. Without this and the forming or active part (according to the high philosophical division into the αἰτιώδης καὶ ὑλικόν [causal and material]), no work, no business, no advancement or foundation.

1. The good painter (*quatenus* painter) begins by working first *within*. Here the imagery! Here the plastic work! First makes forms, fashions, corrects, amplifies, contracts, unites, modifies, assimilates, adapts, conforms, polishes, refines etc., forms his *ideas* : then his hand : his strokes.

2. Thus Raphael, dying young (37). His idea before his hand. All other masters their hand before their idea. He still working to his death. Hand (viz. colouring) scarce come to him ; as painters observe in his best piece of this kind, viz. his Transfiguration, *called* the first picture of the world (this Raphael would have judged otherwise : being mixed, a double piece, not a whole).

3. Accordingly a proficient in this kind (and such a one when found and happening to read this young would thank. me) will apply to his idea, and study invention, for which a real secret (*non obstante*, rehearsal, Mr Bays) viz. passing the forms in review (as soldiers mustering), then checking, redressing, imprinting, stirring, exciting ; then criticizing ; then corroborating[2].

4. And thus the proficient in another science, the true φιλόκαλος [lover of the beautiful], forms his ideas, till a habit (as in Cebes' Table[3], so reiterately enjoined).

The young painter thus becomes original[4], "whilst he

---

[1] Almost not quite so. For judgment will necessarily impart some degree of polishing or working on the forms, species, etc.
[2] See Instinct, p. 105.   [3] *Supra*, pp. 74, 81.
[4] See Characteristics, vol. III, p. 262, note, line 20.

draws from various models," etc. Whereas by copying merely (though this good in some degree and at first) he advances little and can create nothing of his own.

But again the secret (as just above) of invention is (when young) to view good models, etchings (the nearest originals, and really original when by the masters themselves), drawings, cartoons, if not able to come at pictures and statues.

And from hence fleeting forms between sleeping and waking, working on his ambition as well as fancy. So Themistocles haunted and made to walk at nights by the apparitions of the trophies of Miltiades (answerably to the statues[1] said to walk in those days, when many of a family in the house, many in all public places. See Lucian).

From these fleeting forms (call them the effluvia of Epicurus, or the ideas of Plato) the prophet collects still, joins, disjoins, compares, adds, subtracts, modifies, tempers, allays for fear of wildness. Appeal to ordinary fancy of faces upon walls in obscure places where casual lines are drawn at random and chiefly in fever, sickness, or indigestion, grimaces and ugly forms; sometimes fair and beautiful, sometimes bestial, monstrous. These drive away, beat down; those mark, note, remember, raise, repass. So Raphael. So Guido. See their letters. The first of his Galatea or Venus in Pietro Bellori concerning his works. The second in...where he says: "that for the devil (the idea of ugliness) he purposely keeps it out of his mind till necessary to paint." Thus Raphael, a *Raphael*; and Guido, *Guido*.

1. The reverse of this, and the ruin of young artists as well as virtuosos, judges, good eyes and taste, is the contrary habit of not selecting, not gathering; suffering the ideas to present themselves and lead on and engage and enamour as they will or can[2]. No

[1] See what is said bemoaningly of the want of statues, *supra*, p. 108.
[2] See Characteristics, vol. I, p. 312, viz. imperiousness of the *visa*, φαντασίαι, etc.

order: no control: no regulation of the forms: no check, restraint or exception; but all permitted, the appearances—I fancy *ergo* I choose.—I am pleased, therefore, I will be pleased.—But this is impossible: not durable, as in the chosen, select, and truly judicious and natural forms. These durable, eternal, more and more enchanting and instructive, improving, exalting. The other nauseating, soon quelling, satiating: then art and science condemned, slighted. What wonder?

2. 'Tis not the *je ne sais quoi* to which idiots and the ignorant of the art would reduce everything. 'Tis not the δοκεῖ, the I like and you like. But why do I like? And if not with reason and truth I will refuse to like, dislike my fancy, condemn the form, search it, discover its deformity and reject it[1].

2d Part[2] in Painting: Proportion, Drawing, Symmetry particular.

No intention to declare which and which are the proportions; how many heads lengths, whether...or... to a body. (This the Academy, the painter's school, common, practical.) But which and which species, many sorts, even of the heroic genus, still different species,—as Mars more gladiatorian, gregarian, legionary form: thick truss, waist not so noble round, equally turned, as a Hercules of middle age, much less in beauty of form like an Apollo, Bacchus (the true Bacchus), or a Mercury. Witness the best medals as well as statues and ancient relief works.

This founded in nature. For as Hercules (young)

---

[1] [A paragraph follows here in the text numbered 3, beginning: "And thus the proficient," etc. which is the same as 4, *supra*, p. 142 ; and another numbered 4, beginning : "First corruption of taste," etc. which is the same as 2 *supra*, p. 108.]

[2] Note that according to this division into five parts, this second part must be subdivided into two: of which figures (in respect of themselves) must make one, and perspective another.

—No! Not so!—For now I see at least (according to Fréart's report from Junius) that perspective (or optic) must be referred to the last part, viz. collocation.

the finest form to succeed in all the five exercises and carry (as he is said to have done) the prizes of the..., so the form of Mars most proper for war, foot or horse. As *foot* because of the length of the fork, slow marching but gaining ground, not for running. And as *horse*, because of short waist sitting best, and long legs, a help especially when the horse clasped with the calf or shin, as when they used no stirrups to draw and lengthen out their legs, to an inconvenience, if the horse anything low.

Add to this: the thick chestedness for great breath and long endurance of fatigue. The length also of arms (accompanying the long legs) a principal matter in fence by the reach, and in the cast of the lance as well thrust. Also height and tallness generally attending this make more than the longer waisted equal and proportionable. Seldom the well-made and exact bodies seen very tall but middle-sized.

These the reasons for the stated forms of the ancients as they appear in the antiques, and which the practising painters of the Roman schools (present at Rome and studying the antique) learn by rote and do wonderfully, they know not why themselves. And this is the great subject in which Protogenes excelled Apelles by his own confession. This the subject on which the learned artist Euphranor wrote his treatise concerning symmetry, and the different proportions belonging to the different and subdivided under species of the genus MAN[1].

Add to this: " That as the view of the antique, the study of the basso-relievo, statues, etc. (with coins and other assistance) can only be expected to qualify for the right conception of forms in the heroic kind; so this school alone of Rome (whence Raphael, Jul. Romano and Poussin) has as yet ever qualified for the unmixed, pure and simple grace, void of affectation[2].

[1] See Char-cks, I, 144.
[2] Concerning which see in the other head below on the 4th part of painting, i.e. Sentiment, etc.

3rd Part in Painting : viz. Colouring.

Simplicity the main in this, as in all.   But the way to it more strange and paradoxical[1].

The several colours being assembled, and each absolute simple and unmixed in themselves, make in the joint views the least simple and most complex, staring effect that is possible.   Thus patchwork of pure white, red, green, blue, yellow, etc., the more pure, the more ugly; the more simple, the more tawdry—a rainbow, a foolscoat flower, or a real harlequin foolscoat, a parrot, peacock, jay, *pictaeque volucres* (as Virgil calls them).   Nature's painting! But nature not to be painted where she herself paints. Not a picture of a picture.

This the simplicity which delights children[2].   Gaudy, striking.   " Itself a spectacle not a medium by which other spectacles, views are created, raised, exhibited." Colours the instruments, not the subject-matter. Means: not end.   Imitation, lesson, instruction, pedagogy of the eye : to make it learned, erudite, polite, acute, judicious in its choice and discernment of objects; in its fruition of beauty, its taste of good, by which its pleasure consistent and lasting, and by which by easy transition the mind learns its art and fruition : the moral pictures known and proportion discovered.

Thus in respect of painting and the art of imitation by colours, the least simple, sincere and genuine, etc. in the cloth or seam of the tablature are those which are the most simple, pure and absolute in themselves. These the true art of painting abhors.

Nor would a Raphael, a Jul. Romano, a Titian (the chief in this), endure such a glare, notwithstanding the Pietro da Cortona and other corrupters, with all the French, Poussin excepted.   A mere white, a mere

---

[1] *Infra*, p. 149.
[2] Such the bubbles of soap-suds blown up by children and ravishing, first for their regular figure (as the globe, the cube, the cylinder, etc., in Moralists), and next for their colouring, the various and rich.

scarlet, a mere blue[1], (the worst of all and most abused because of the *lapis lazuli*, and Pliny's reason of the rich fancy of the great, and ruin of painting) all these so many monarchies or monarchs, independent, absolute. Now nothing should be so as to colouring in the piece. The ambient air and earth (being chief of the field or camps) govern chiefly, and then the greater bodies. To the air or sky belong the clouds, and all the tints which the painter thinks fit to raise out of them, as he may to best advantage, whatever he pleases, in great variety. To the other part, viz. the earth, belong the rocks, ruins, pieces of architecture, trees, rivers, pools, broken grounds of all sorts, out of which also the painter may, for the interest and economy of his figures, raise what variety of tints he can find occasion or thought to use.

Next to these two fundamental repositories, come the great and near figures themselves with the great draperies, whether on or off of the bodies. All these[2] as they receive so they communicate to each other. The sky chiefly to these; but these again something to those, and much to one another. For every considerable mass which carries light, every illuminated and coloured body in a picture, is a chameleon and borrows something. Everything[3] gives and takes and from this multiplicity of tints is formed that chief and amiable simplicity, the very perfection of colouring.

[1] An azure blue for this reason also one of the worst of colours, as it robs heaven, kills the sky, puts the very celestial bodies out of countenance, hills, sea, waters, etc., and which if any might tend to simplicity and absoluteness; but yet how false see in Gaspar and the best perspective painters.

The ultra marine or *lapis lazuli*, good (they say) to hold the colouring. Excellent. Therefore use, but mix, allay, change, break and modify it.

[2] *Supra*, p. 118.

[3] For this reason a mass of blue draperies red, rose, yellow, etc., not sufferable; because it must communicate too much and can take or receive but little or nothing. For how go about to break such a bright original and wrongly-simple mass? Above all, blue the worst.

Mariage[1] des Couleurs.   Contrapposizione[2] della Tinta.

1. Melting of colours, symphony, harmony. Age
helping a picture, why but for this reason ? Ridiculous!
When we can have that effect instantly and without
loss (for age loses and in the shades or sinkings,
expression vanishes). But we see with a false and
artificial eye what is new, and expect the *new* genius,
the mere *paint*, and wont believe ourselves that when
colours are finest, work is worst. As if old music
(were this possible) could pass when heard simple, but
new music the contrary. Or as if music was to be set
at a distance and half of it drowned, lost and unheard,
that the other half might be the more music and more
harmonious. Ridiculous! As if music near at hand
and all in hearing (and so picture all in sight) could
not be so governed and modulated as to hear all that
should be heard. Thus the glare and gloss of new
painting once off, i.e. when but once thoroughly dry :
nothing else can add, if painted according to plastic
truth. But that, the modern painter, though a
Raphael, (a Poussin chiefly), fears to do. So he must
wait for time hereafter and be really better seen then
(when perished in part even in his picture), than in
his own time and in the perfection of his work. For
if perchance he ventures to paint perfect and right at
first, antiquity alone (the name of it) must give it
protection. Its own merit cannot, and the painter
must be condemned for doing well, because he is
modern : because the modern taste is false ; and
affectation of antiquity alone sets us right in ancient
pieces.

I remember in the working of a sketch once by a

---

[1] Hence may be used poetically, and in the style of this treatise, the
expressions of the ambition of colours, their aspiring, assuming, their
encroachment on the art, their domineering, their insolence, pride,
avarice (because of gold and silver, jewels, etc., intermixt and what Pliny
says, Char-cks, I, p. 340), as well as that riot and luxury, luxuriant.

[2] Hence in opposition, maquerellage, libertinage, prostitution, as it
were fornication, whoredom of colours, unlawful procreation, engendering,
copulating, spurious race, bastardy, illegitimacy.

good master in history to have seen all run harmoniously, and colours embrace, love, etc., when on
a sudden a fine cherry-colour clapt in made the same
painful harsh effect, as a trumpet putting in on a
sudden, with a soft mellow voice and a theorbo lute in
a chamber.

2. Remember here the story of the deaf man's
likening scarlet to a trumpet.

3. Strange paradox[1]! but leading maxim, viz.
"that in tablature and painting, colours are in themselves nothing, nor have nothing to do." For first
all the perfect and true rejected as wholly false in the
workmanship. The rest dirtied, deadened, mixed,
confounded, and as it were annihilated. The slave
of all.

Remember censure[2] of cartoons: viz. Raphael's
druggery[3] for hangings. This a fatal stumbling block
of taste for English-men, being our great model, if no
caution and premonition. All gaudiness, all false.
The very pattern of falsehood. Curious to see how
all turned together (bad music!) by so good a master,
so prostitute to cardinals, popes, etc.

Maxim[4]. That: "By as much as they attract to
themselves, by so much they detract and derogate
from the design, and render the execution of the piece
defective and impotent." For if glaring colours in the
standing frame or close about the picture disturb the
view, and weaken the strength of our imagination on
which the painter practises and to which he chiefly
applies, what effect must these colours have when
introduced into the piece itself? And how is that
attention likely to be commanded which is necessary
for that pleasing illusion or deceit which makes the
sole use and beauty of the spectacle? 'Tis evident
that in the pieces of *claro-obscuro*, but especially where

---

[1] *Supra*, p. 148.   [2] *Supra*, p. 118.
[3] [Possibly the nature of drugget.]
[4] On the subject of florid colours taken from maxim at the end of the
Treatise II, viz. The Notion.

a single colour is added, if the design and history be well performed, the illusion becomes so strong, and the eye of the able spectator so fixed, and by a sort of enchantment in a manner riveted to the subject: that the mind in its first transports requires not anything further; nor does the fancy while this fervour lasts suggest the least defect, or suffer the least uneasiness for want of what is still behind. How must it prove, therefore, when the whole force of colours, under a just management and due restraint are added to the piece? And how real an enchantment must be then produced when all the resemblances of nature in her proper aspects are assembled and united harmoniously and in consort to complete the summary and the supreme work of art?

The Modern Four Colours.

The modern four colours, viz. 1. Terra rossa. Ocre rouge. 2. Terra galla. Ocre jaune. 3. Oltra-marino. Azuro. Lapis lazuli. 4. Terra verde, de verona ferrigno, iron-coloured. The light and dark, viz. 1. Biacca y ceruse. Blanc de plomb. Ceruse. 2. Terra nigra. The last has also a dun colour akin to it to be called Terra d'ombra. The green, however, seems not an original, or principal colour, since it can be made by mixture of black and yellow with a little white. A few hints only of this kind to be proved by others. This a foundation or *ansa* [handle] only. Our consideration and work different.

It must be remarked upon the whole, after the small explanation (not too precise or mechanical) of the four colours that: this was meant by the four colours of Apelles, etc., in Pliny. Not merely by four without the mixture and result.

Remember also here the reigning tint[1] or regent colour, master species. The real complexion from the chief in the complex, the predominant in the

[1] Tint 4.

assemblage and mixture. This to be explained by the easy practice of a curtain of any one colour drawn before the single window or entrance of light into a room. Be there what colours it will, it instantly reduces them all and forms one of those species of drawings reckoned amongst the claro obscuros—amongst which is an old way of a particular colour as yellow or dun added to the black and white, which makes three colours, though in strictness but one colour, the other black and white, being shade and light only, not colouring : not a piece said to be in colours on this account, nor indeed on the addition of this one real colour, though green, blue or red. This being still in the singular not plural. But when a real second colour is super-added, a progeny arises as from male and female, and the parents beget abundantly. Good reason therefore to stop at four. For see how multiplied a generation! Though kindred and so affectionately, kindly, consan-guineously allied and united. Therefore live the ancients.

4th Part in Painting: viz. Sentiment, Movement, Passion, Soul.

The divine part and only Raphael's. Something which is above the modern turn and only antique species of grace. Above the dancing-master, above the actor and the stage. Above the other masters of exercise. And this even the ordinary painters and statuarys see ; and therefore, no toe twisted out, no chin held up. No stalk[1], or tread, or bridling, like the tragic, or theatrical action. Yet the sneer retained ; the twist ; the affected contrast. " Here and here. This way and this way." So the French modern school, in reverse of Poussin their renegade ; or rather they his rebels, since he had a right to be their prince.

---

[1] No seat, a horse-buck, according to modern discipline and ac-coutrements, stirrups, etc., with raised chin, tossing head, etc.

This an eternal distinction between ancient and modern. The first ever without affectation. The latter (except Raphael, Poussin, and in statuary Michael Angelo) all give into it more or less. And the cavalier Bernini[1] in this respect an apostate in statuary, as Pietro da Cortona in painting, both for this and for colours[2].

Definition of *affectation*, viz. "An expressed consciousness of grace which spoils grace and its simplicity. An attention to self, to the action, movement, or attitude itself." This unpardonable even in a Venus, and never allowed even there by the ancients.

Many ill works remaining of ancients (for must not they have had their underlings and botches as well as we?). But never a show or token of this affectation in coin, basso relievo, statue, etc.

5th Part in Painting: viz. System, Composition[3], Collocation, Position, Symmetry general.

Hyperbole[4]. 1. In this part treat of the magistrates (together with the hyperbole), e.g. In portraitures, even in half-lengths and heads, often a window open and a distant perspective of small and lessened objects, no way, not by any medium or middle size united to the great. This a plain breach of symmetry, and an errour in the magnitudes.

[1] Memd. Bernini wicked. Therefore sit the harder on him as on Spaniolet, Carvagio, etc., throwing in a word in behalf of M. Angelo and Salvator Rosa. This elsewhere not here.

[2] See Colouring.

[3] Beware of word composition here, since it may be applied equivocally to Invention, part 1st.

[4] On the subject of the hyperbole (which I believe will require a distinct head) remember principally the noble ancient statue of Laocoon. True example! But so unknown to modern judges, that it is even condemned by critics, as if the master, great as he was, had been such a blunderer as to mistake his sizes, and give the form of twenty or twenty one years old to a pair of children, not half grown. N.B. This is the very statue (of which I have the old print), a good subject for Mr Frei. Gribelin, or other engraver in little; to fit the octavo size and stand in the page under this chapter, among the ornaments of Second Characters.

The same rule holds as well in the masses or groups as between the particular pieces or figures.

2. By the very use of the hyperbole (which is a voluntary and premeditated errour from the rules of perspective) those very rules are shown to be most necessary for the painter to understand. The deviation *in loco* requiring the nicest knowledge and reason. As for instance when it is and how a distant figure on a ground near the horizon (the air appearing under its legs), or receiving a strong light on any extremity or particular part, comes to be excessive and large beyond its proportion, as in N. Poussin's figure and perspective piece of the Samaritan Woman, where a pointing finger is longer than the whole head or face.

How agreeable this part! (essential and constituent of piece and tablature) even when found in ryparography, animals, a dunghill (cock and hens), a flower, or fruit piece (according to what delivered in Notion at paragraph 3 of the introduction) if perchance the poor master has a genius of this kind ; and has order in his head, to him indeed the *je ne sais quoi* yet perceived and executed. *Il ne sait comment*: ravishes and delight others. *Ils ne savent pourquoi.*

15. MAXIMS OF THE ART[1].

1. A tablature must have but one point of sight.

2. It must be seen only from one position, or point of sight, and be so wrought that if nearer or further viewed, it appears imperfect. For if as well nearer or further, here or there: then as well no-where. The touches or pencil (as well as the dimensions in fresco-work and uneven superficies) must trim the balance and drive you back, or bring you forward, as your eye (you will find) requires.

3. All very little painting (viz. less than natural

---

[1] Mem[d]. The only [section] which is to be marked with hands (as determined above, p. 7). Bring first as many as possible into the first Treatises, and mark them still repeatedly with the hands afterwards, both there and here.

lessening at convenient distance computed within and without the tabula or cloth) is false ; and only sufferable in portraiture of faces, not whole or half-figures ; which would be still so much the more preposterous as being *more*, and the *littleness* amplified and more apparent and resulting pigmy, baby-forms.   But in this respect (if history and real humanity) false : because no life so lessened can appear so distinct, or features be seen and counted.   Therefore bemoan the excellent Poussin employing the greatest truth of pencil and judgment in a kind or species that is in itself false, but for cabinets—and so he got his livelihood best—: modesty and the great masters all before him discouraging him from the noble size and that above life, of which otherwise so capable.   Witness his...in St Peter's.   But his pieces of two or three feet, not of the kind here censured.   These excellent. His Plague and other pieces in the French king's closet of the unhappy little kind, and relish of closet virtuosos and the court.

Hyperbole.

In the heroic style (as either epic or tragic) the hyperbole[1] has place and must reign : else no heroes, no amplification.   And therefore buskin (*cothurnus*) high raised, bigger than life, voice and tone suitable, and action (which makes the strut and bellow endured even to extravagance in the actor).   But in the common, practical, and merely natural style, the hyperbole runs to farce immediately and the buskins are stilts ; the tones whining or bellowing in reality. The descriptions, motions, etc. are Horace's ' Dwarf of Augustus in Arms.'   The genuine comic becomes farce ;   the middle comedy and Menander, Aristophanic.

Even the great Michael Angelo[2], his muscling

---

[1] *Supra*, p. 100.
[2] Confer with Sensus Communis, p. 144 notes.

action and movements gigantic. Other painters too timorous and strict; sweet and natural; but unfit for any noble sally of genius, as Domenichino the judicious, correct, and Poussin. And among the yet more modern, Carlo Marat, fittest for beauty and soft action; not fierce, terrible. So wrong was a certain Cardinal's judgment, who having two contrary pieces to bespeak, a tragic ugly one, and a pleasant beautiful one, gave the former to Salvator Rosa and the latter to Marat. Whence this absurdity: "The devils or furies of the latter were angel's forms; the angels of the former furies."

Of the happy medium and just hyperbole, see perpetual instance in divine Raphael. And here cite[1] and reprove sharply the sharp French censurer and railer Fréart[2] particularly p. 47 being the exact description and very picture of the false taste. Nothing being so just and beautiful on this very account as Raphael's in this Massacre of the Innocents (of which I have seen the original drawing).

Again as to the hyperbole even in perspective— Salvator Rosa[3]: "He had chosen a cloth of a vast height in proportion to its breadth. It was full...by... This was with design to compose his perspective of huge parts (according to the right and noble taste), taking in for the purpose as much height as was possible for his near rocks and trees which would require it; and choosing to lose the shapeliness of his piece both as to frame and portion of space without, and as to the whole or body within, rather than not approach his great objects of this kind; which could not therefore be seen to their tops if so mighty a height had not been gained.

"Accordingly when this was done he introduced his

---

[1] In the notes.
[2] Fréart's *An Idea of the Perfection of Painting*. Preface at the end of p. 14. Bigot, revenge against M. Angelo.
[3] A small history of this Salvator Rosa which though no where written or told and though past long before my time (for he died ere I was born). I shall relate as if had been present.

rock in the most stupendous manner. This being designed and drawn to his fancy; he proceeds to adorn his piece (according to his natural ambition) with those wild savage figures of banditti, wandering gypsies, strollers, vagabonds, etc., at which he was so excellent; and being pushed on still by that vanity to make these also in great perfection and to advantage, he designed and painted them on a forward ground, in a full size or rather larger than naturally the perspective would allow at so near a distance. He had no sooner done this than he perceived what injury he had done at the same time to his first design and that after doing all in his power to magnify his rock and raise the majesty and grandeur of that form and principal part, he had pulled it back again, thrown it off to a distance, or what was worse, kept it in the same place but rendered it diminutive, which in that peculiar form and shape of horrour and dismay would prove a sort of burlesque and absolutely ridiculous (like a little elephant, a little camel, etc.). This was the faulty *reiterate* hyperbole, which destroys itself put all out of tune and order, and renders the whole fantastical and a mere vision, a sick dream, not a clear view, an inviting, instructive, exalting fiction or poem.

"But what does Salvator upon this. In an instant, ere the paint was well laid, he strikes all out with a dash or two of his pencil, destroys his giants niched in his hollow cave, and draws a rock over his vast abode, as Dryden translates in his Proteus of Virgil's Eclogues. But that his piece might not want its ornamental human figures he immediately upon a yet nearer ground places just such another figure or two at least three sizes less, by which his hyperbole once again came right, the grandeur of parts in perspective restored, and his rock majestic, terribly impending, vast, enormous; as it should be, and as he first designed it."

The picture (with another of the same kind, its fellow) was purchased at a high price by the truly great and worthy Prince and Governour, the Viceroy of Naples; after whose death, his pictures coming to sale, the piece mentioned, together with its fellow, came into the hands of the author. And the piece mentioned being set in a counter light sufficiently discovers the passage related.

Great maxim of colouring[1], viz. "For the hyperbole something must be sacrificed." Therefore, see what? The hyperbole must be *one*, only one, unique, simple.

Upon the same subject of hyperbole apply Horace's[2] *Qui nil molitur inepte* ["who begins with no foolish effort"]. So the divine Raphael in this respect far beyond Michael Angelo, whose figures labour and toil though without reason, showing great learning in design, anatomy, etc., but without cause. But particularly among the more modern Pietro da Cortona, who often *molitur inepte*, overdoes in this sense, as in his colouring and ornaments, overrich, magnificent, false.

Ellipsis[3].

1. From the following two maxims, viz. (1) "*Frustra fit per plura*," etc., confirmed in practice by nature in anatomy; and (2) "whatever in poetic or plastic imitation, or rhetoric, is left to guess and results strong and striking though not expressed" (as by the figure ellipsis)—from these two maxims, I say, this deduction: That the outline when skipped, or lost (as in an arm running over any part of the body, and marked only here and there), and yet has its effect at due distance, shows the power of art, and has its suitable effect even on the unconscious spectator.

2. Remember the ellipsis (or omission, retrenchment, reform, reduction) of the traces and harness in the divinity and triumphal chariots, and even racing chariots, ploughs, etc., in medal and antique relief-work entails, etc.: yet this however to be moderated in

---

[1] See above, p. 149.
[2] Horace's *De Arte Poetica*, l. 140.
[3] Outline *see* Free-manner, *infra*, p. 165.

painting and colours, because of the maxim in Notion
(chap. v, par. 12).

3. In the comparison between poetry and painting
(1st and 2d Characters) this difference: That what
may decently be described in one not seen the least
in the other; so in a plague painted[1], mascerated bodies
and cadaverous looks indicative of the sores, but no
plain sore, no running boil, or plague-sore, no ulcer,
cancer, or the like. From hence argument *a fortiori*:
How indecent is obscenity? When painting in other
impurities is so nice and cannot show what may be
said in the broadest, harshest terms.

4. Again of the ellipsis and outline. The sense
as well as the wit and fancy loves to guess, when easy;
hates to be overhelped, tutored. In leaping, running,
to take a leap, aiming at a thrust in fencing, a recurring
to the rule puzzles. The fruit of the doctrine to be
from nature and instinct, no lesson applied or thought
of at the time. Besides that in views whether real or
imitative, that which is gathered from a few characteristics, or notes, principal aspects, touches, lines,
features, is more powerfully gathered[2], more simply
formed in the conception, idea, more distinct and firmly
lodged in the memory, and sealed to the sense or
understanding, than what is multifariously drawn from
a confusion of concurrent indicatives, which destroy
the effect of each other. So in rhetoric and a cause
pleaded, the one reason or the two or three principal
grounds well urged; the rest slighted. Else the fine
speech and the enforced argument overturns the cause;
shows the fine grammarian and logician, but destroys
the orator. Not so Demosthenes, who having struck
his blow, etc. So the tragedians, epics, enemies of the
detail as all great arts. And so the great masters in
their style of painting, hate minuteness[3].

[1] *Supra*, p. 141.
[2] *lecta potenter*. Horace's *De Arte Poetica*, l. 40, and what ensues
by way of facility in the artist's free pencil. *Verbaque provisam rem non
invita sequentur*, l. 311.
[3] See Characteristics, I, 144.

The power of the figure and its supreme utmost politeness well known to those who have studied the ancient critics and orators as well as poets, with what has been remarked on the style of Isocrates, Demosthenes[1], etc. Even in comedy a Menander, a Terence. Ego ne illam, quae illum, quae me, quae non? So even a La Fontaine in his first fable[2], etc., *par le moindre petit morceau*, which shows that author (who prostituted his muse and lost his real beauty and simplicity in his long, multiform, complex, unshapely tales, where the ill salt and lewdness chiefly attracts (carmina Lucilii[3])) to have imbibed the ancient wit and to have known more of true dialogue than Fontenel, whose dialogues of the dead are only tricked with patch work, commonplace book writing without body[4], grace or characters. And a single fable of La Fontaine will, both with the lady page and the philosopher, be read (sincerely speaking) more repeatedly again and again at all hours and times, than the finest of his ancient masqueraders whom he defames and defaces, and are indeed real marks and speeches. No one of the real good judges of the French but would avow they had rather be author of one such little fable as this of the ant and the grasshopper (where characters and manners are touched, and the very spirit and humour of the housewifely dame and frugal man of business and the prodigal squire are exactly touched)

---

[1] Remember to search Longinus for this, also Dionysius Halicarnassus, and what Aristotle says above all; and let this be a full and large note of citations.

[2] So the omission of the two indicatives of the dialogue in the last line, as in all his dialogue manner : a thing of the nicest judgment and art, to know when and how to omit ; of which Horace the great pattern after his masters in Greece.

[3] [This word is obscure in the text.]

[4] See Char-cks (upon the manner of dialogue writing), Vol. I, p. 196. And what is said of the same false manner of dialogue writing used by certain divines and other false imitators of Plato and the ancients. These dialogues of Monsieur Fontenel being indeed only bad imitations of a bad false imitator Lucian, good only in style and humour of the lower of the abusive 1st comedy and his master mimic Aristophanes : the great paroder and only model of what we call burlesque, and was quitted in the middle ages of politeness, viz. from Aristophanes to this Lucian.

than of either of the volumes of that other author's
uncharacterized characters, and dialogues of phantoms
with borrowed names and without a tale or story,
a moral design, draught, or any proportion, body or
shape belonging to them. This author is worthy,
however, of criticism, being one who was able to write
well, as his dialogue of the *Pluralite des Mondes* may
serve to show, where there is some kind of imitation
(with allowance for modern air of gallantry): the
chief and common scope, mark, or butt of dialogue
and poetry, and all fictitious work according to
Atheneus in Char-cks, 1, 254, and so 196, Homer, etc.

16. OF THE MACHINE, MACHINERY, OR DEITY WORK.

Deus intersit. Always necessary in the high heroic
(as in the epic). No piece sublime without the action
being in this respect of full dignity. Dignus Vindicis
Nodus. No tablature complete in the heroic kind
without.

Ergo common history (though of heroes such as
Alexander, Caesar, Mark Antony, etc.) not of the
higher epic order in painting; because no machine
introducible, and much less modern history (except in
the emblematic and oblique way, which is of the
irregular kind) since a King William, a Louis, can
much less appear in the field, or council, with a train of
deities, or with Mars, Minerva, Apollo, Mercury, etc.

But when the Christian machine enters (as in the
case of a Constantine), then the painter again rises
and heroism complete, the miraculous and sublime
restored with credibility, through faith, tradition, sacred
history, religion, as in heathenism, and the ancient
machine.

Ergo fable more the subject of historical painting
than mere history. Same reasons as in poetry. See
Char-cks, Aristotle and places depending.

This is besides the advantages of the machine, the

glory's, clouds, and miraculous lights as Apollo in particular : the rays about his head as the sun ; and something of this kind in proportion also to other deitys and demigods.

But why ancient machine still superiour to modern, see example in such a case as the weakness of human nature, or the virile virtue in opposition to the female charms or those of love. Take a Hercules (according to the common fiction) and an Omphale. Here the hero spins, lies in the lap, etc. Cupids above and below triumph, insult, illude. Venus laughs. Even fawns and satyrs may come in to make sport and add to the victory since the same fiction makes Hercules withal subject to the pleasure of wine and of the table. Now change the scene and take a Samson. What machine ? Not angels surely. And for demons much less. How would this appear ? Ergo moderns hit the sublime best in the more ghastly and (otherwise) ungraceful *in-venuste* subject of executioners and martyrs, or hideous dying pieces, beggary, prayer, etc. As Domenichino instance the second esteemed picture in the world (according to Poussin, etc.), viz. St Jerome taking the host. A sacred mystery, seen with the eyes of faith and confirmed by the very machine above. All noble ! and exalting low part.

Nothing worse than the unskilful mixture and confusion of the machine work with the historical and human figures. A delicate and just perceptible distinction and separation necessary. Not so as to make two pieces, or two styles, or two sorts of light (though somewhat of this latter kind not amiss if well united by intermediates).

Examine Raphael's Transfiguration piece by this maxim, and observe how the false double piece (viz. the part above) serves however as the machine part with an infinite advantage.

Remember Rubens' Mercury with the two cardinals and queen, as an instance of the monstrous mixture of machine and history...Luxembourg gallery, Paris.

17. Of the Scene, Camps, Perspective, Ornament.

(1) Of landscape painting or perspective considered by itself.

> Ego laudo ruris amoeni
> Rivos et musco circumlita saxa, nemusque[1].

["I praise the streams, the moss-covered rocks and the groves of the delightful country."]

Also that of Juvenal after encomiums of the country in his own way.   Satire 3 in the beginning and the

> *Ego vel Prochytam praepono Suburae.*
> In vallem Egeriae descendimus, et speluncas
> Dissimiles veris.   Quanto praestantius esset
> Numen aquae, viridi si margine clauderet undas
> Herba, nec ingenuum violarent marmora tophum?

["*I prefer even Prochyta to the Suburra.* We descended into the valley of the Egeria and the grottoes so altered from what nature made them. How much more should we feel the influence of the presiding genius of the spring, if turf enclosed the waters with its margin of green, and no marble profaned the native stone."]

And that of the other severe poet (for even the severest allow and even exalt this relish as the truly natural.   So we see in this of Juvenal in order from that foot or foundation to reproach and shame vice, and at being in itself divine and moral[2] according to the spirit of the Lucilius's, the Horace's, etc.), viz. Persius, Sat. 6.

> Hybernatque meum mare[3], qua latus ingens
> Dant scopuli et multa litus se valle receptat.

[1] Hor. *Epist.* Lib. I, X. 6.
[2] Characteristics, I, 141.
[3] So Horace's description of his villa :
    Continui montes, nisi dissocientur opacâ
    Valle ; ...
and   Paulum silvae super his.
and   Ubi ingens pinus albaque populus
    Umbram hospitalem, etc. et obliquo laborat lympha.

[And my sea is wintry, where the rocks present a large side, and the shore recedes into a deep valley.]

Hic ego securus vulgi, etc.

[" Here am I, careless of the vulgar."]

These are the images with which a mind must be filled ; these the beauties of which it must be apprised and with which it must be enamoured and possessed, previously to this taste in painting.   For so in poetry. What would pastorals (for instance) prove to one who had no relish of the real *paysage* ? the *rus*, animals, and rural objects.

Remember the several orders (as of old with Mr Clost^r in Richmond Park and St Giles's woods) into which it is endeavoured to reduce the natural views : the last and most sacred, like the Alpine kind, where the vast wood and caverns with the hollows and deep valleys worn by the cataracts in the very rock itself, pines, firs, and trunks of other aged trees[1].   This attempted by Salvator Rosa, but without the just speculation.   Witness the stickiness of his noble trees (which he otherwise finely described), and his mangling them like artificial trunks and amputations made by man and with instruments—contrary to the idea of those sacred recesses, where solitude and deep retreat, and the absence of gainful, lucratible and busy mortals, make the sublime, pathetic and enchanting, raises the sweet melancholy, the revery, meditation.   "Where no hand but that of time.   No steel, no scythe, but that of Saturn's."   Secret[2] suggestion of the world's ruin and decay ; its birth and first formation[3], "where neither art nor the conceit or caprice of man has spoiled their genuine order[4]."

[1] See Rhapsody, p. 389, etc.
[2] Against the atheists of the world (this globe's eternity).
[3] Cf. Rhapsody, pp. 389—390 and 393, line 22.
[4] Write this fluently, though a repetition of what writ before in Rhapsody to which no occasion to refer here purposely.   For why not cite one's own when suitable, as Xenophon (his battle of Mantinea in his Agesilaus and his History), after Homer and the poets.   So Lucretius, Virgil.   If moderns imitate not, 'tis because not so elaborate, just.   On 'Self-citation,' *supra*, p. 4.

18.   OF SHORTENINGS OR FORE-SHORTENING.

All the shortenings of figures, or other constituent
parts of the tablature our painters have customarily
called by the name of fore-shortenings because indeed
all shortenings of a particular single figure (standing
by itself and being substantial not adjective, but containing the point of sight within itself) are indeed
fore-shortenings, that is, shortenings, foresight. But
the point of sight being taken out of the figure and
removed to some other (which changes the whole
economy of the tablature), the shortenings whatever
they are become quite different; though the attitude of
that figure be exactly the same. The whole drawing
is then changed, be the figure transplanted but a half
body's breadth either to the one side or other, or
removed but a faces' length either higher or lower in
respect of the horizon, which must be the first thing
fixed even by the most stupid and paltry draughtsman
before he can draw so much as a man at table, a dish
on it, a dog under it. For if the point of sight be just
above the table so that the dish be seen into, if the
servant raises the dish it must be seen by the bottom
and no possibility of seeing into it; unless the point of
sight again be raised higher and the horizon supposed
above the raised dish; and then the bottom dishes are
not only deeper seen into, but the guests' heads are seen
like the dishes before, and their crowns or upper parts
discovered, chins and throats so much lost in proportion.
The same side-ways, right and left, whence may rise
the phrase, high-shortening; low-shortening; side-
shortening.

19.   OF TRUTH (viz. PLASTIC).

Remember what argued with Mr Trench about my
design of the good and evil conscience (two boys) for
flourish plate of Treatise III of Characteristics. The
harpies and evil dreams in volatile shapes, being first

proposed to be made bigger than the life in respect of
the boys, that their action and accompaniments might
be seen the plainer.   But this was found nought and
false.   Afterwards having reduced them to as big as
life, but having chosen rather the eagle and vulture-
proportion as the largest: this still was found false.
For at this rate, the haggard forms instead of buffeting
and frightening the children might be supposed big
enough to fly away with them as their prey.   The next
size therefore was chosen, viz. that of the raven, the
kite, etc.

This merely in grotesque work and the emblematic;
where all is false and everything so wildly and ex-
travagantly fictitious, with such variety of proteus-
forms and different species conjoined; yet not pre-
posterously, absurdly, or without intelligence, speculation and a truth!

—Non ut placidis coëant immitia[1].

["Not to join what's fierce with what is mild."]
How great a testimony to truth and support of that
early maxim in Characteristics, 1, p. 4, "That truth
is the most powerful thing in the world."   So again,
pp. 142, 146 of Sensus Communis.

And here by the way take notice in relation to
Horace's verse just cited, that the harpy form is no
objection to him.   Since if the fair lady was joined
to the vulture beneath, this was the more moral and
instructive, like the other forms of the siren-kind, to
show the speciousness of vice, and that in such
characters the best countenance and face of sweetness
and beauty may hide the greatest cruelty underneath,
and be joined to the most savage disposition.

20.   Of Freedom or the Free Manner.

1.   Remember Mgr Heer Van der Werff (the exact
contrary) his Abraham, Sarah, and Hagar introduced.

---

[1] Hor. *De Arte Poet.* l. 12.

All false, bound up, glued, clung, candied, baked....And withal minute, contracted, diminished, miniatured, particularized, detailed, little parts expressed, nails, hair, etc. (as ridiculed by Horace in the Émilian Faber. See Char-cks). No sacrifice of under parts, no subjection of tints, beating down the ambitious colours[1]. No introducing of the mortifying kind (*amortir* in French), no abatement, degradation; consequently, no elevation, exaltation, or sublime. No hyperbole, majesty, etc. No.[2]....And lastly no ellipsis or right direction in the outline[3].

Compare the ellipsis in the outline of painting to the superficies of large or colossus statuary work, or relief work set at a distance. For here the roughness helps. Remarkable lineaments and no more. Not the Emilian Faber. Not the hairs. But by this rule: "That whatever is hid by the due distance, whether in painting or statuary, is not only superfluous, but injurious and detracting."

Remember the Ephesian colossus[4] (of which Salvator Rosa speaks in his satire on painting), which being admired before erected, was afterwards found to lose much instead of gaining as was believed.

Also Pliny's story of Nero's passion for a statue, which he first gilded (by which he gave dazzling lights and odd reflections to the before quiet, passive, and sober work); then ungilt by scraping off, whence besides a small diminution of each part of the superficies (and not in proportion neither) he made all smooth, and could not possibly without new impression and subtraction restore to its original roughness and masculine touch and complexion.

2. Freedom! Free-manner! What? As how? Why not explain? This said by everyone. But let us hear what account? Few except the painter can give any. And the painter mute in this respect viz. that he has neither language nor pen by which to

---

[1] See in Colours, *supra*, p. 148.   [2] *Supra*, p. 155.
[3] *Supra*, p. 159.   [4] Quere where to find this story?

explain himself clearly to those who are not of the mystery and trade. (Not so the ancient painters, who wrote and philosophized on their art.) Thus certain philosophers coiffed in their artificial terms of ideas, complex, reflex, etc., are angry when they cannot explain their mind to one without the pale[1].

3. Concerning freedom see a moral explanation: The same doctrine and explanation of liberty and freedom in true moral philosophy as in painting, viz. "That the truly austere, severe, and self-severe, regular, restraintive, character and regimen corresponds (not fights or thwarts) with the free, the easy, the secure, the bold. τὸ θαρσἄλέον [the undaunted]," etc. "Not libertinism for liberty." No libertinage, dissoluteness, but the only ἐλευθερία [freedom]. Sibi qui imperiosus[2] [who controls himself].

4. Memorandum. In life of Titian, what he said upon his loose, wild strokes over the hair anu complection of a portraiture nicely painted, viz. that he did it por coprire la fatica, to cover the fatigue, or bury the pains.

21. OF THE DECORUM.

This the place for censure of the censurer of Raphael Monsieur Fréart[3]. But then by way of excuse for him (he being a stout defender of the ancients) observe: "That this is in common with all other popish virtuosi accustomed to cruel and indecent spectacles...Painting, wholly opposite to the decorum, viz. crucifixion, martyrdoms, wheels, gibbets, torments, to be ranked indeed in ryparography.

A painter therefore must imitate the dramatic and scenical, not the epic and merely recitative poet.

---

[1] See the parallel place in the divine man.
[2] Cf. Horace, Sat. II. vii. 83. So Char-ks (Miscellany, p. 311 and other passages).
[3] As above, p. 132.

See Homer's (*Iliad* XVIII, 569) description of Achilles shield :

(1) Τοῖσιν δ' ἐν μέσσοισι πάϊς φόρμιγγι λιγείῃ
Hos vero inter medios puer etiam cithara sonora
Ἱμερόεν κιθάριζε, λίνον δ' ὑπὸ καλὸν ἄειδεν
Suaviter citharicabat chorda autem belle resonabat
Λεπταλέῃ φωνῇ· τοὶ δὲ ῥήσσοντες ἁμαρτῇ
Tenella voce hic hiero pulsantes terram simul
Μολπῇ τ' ἰυγμῷ τε ποσὶ σκαίροντες ἕποντο.
Cantuque sibiloque pedibus tripudiantes seque-
bantur.

["And in the midst of them a boy made pleasant music on a clear toned viol, and sang thereto a sweet Linos-song with delicate voice ; while the rest with feet falling together kept time with music and song."]

And so again Virgil's description of Aeneas' shield. The wolf nurse: Illam tereti cervice reflexa mulcere alternos[1]. ["She with sleek neck bent back stroked them by turns."]

Nec non Tarquinium ejectum Porsenna jubebat
Accipere....
Aeneadae in ferrum pro libertate ruebant[2].

["Therewithal Porsenna commanded to admit the exiled Tarquin.
The Aeneadae rushed on the sword of liberty."]

Here we have tyranny and liberty painted but without marks or signature, and so huzzas and the noise of multitudes. Laetitia ludisque viae plausuque fremebant[3]. ["The streets were loud with gladness and games and cheering."] And even variety of language, victae longo ordine gentes, quam variae linguis, habitu tam vestis et armis[4]. ["The conquered tribes move in long line, diverse, as in tongue, so in fashion, in dress, and in armour."]

These two works are real spectacles, not recitals of

---

[1] Virgil's *Aeneid*, VIII. 633.   [2] *Ibid.* 646.
[3] *Ibid.* 717.   [4] *Ibid.* 723.

spectacles, where the mind takes in greedily what the
eye cannot (1) investigate, or (2) endure.

Thus Medea, whether in the scene or the chaste
correct tablature, must not actually stab her children
(coram populo[1]); but the combat of the passion must
be seen and represented according to supreme art, not
the butchery and mere event and fact.

Thus ever in battles (heroic and of good masters),
rarely a spear sticking in a body, and then too not in
a principal or near figure.   Never a head divided like
that by Turnus in the *Aeneid*[2].

(2)   Atque illi partibus aequis
Huc caput atque illuc humero ex utroque pependit.

["In equal halves
The sundered head from either shoulder swung."]
And just before

Et mediam ferro gemina inter tempora frontem
Dividit, impubesque immani vulnere malas[3].

["Clove temples, brows and beardless cheeks clean
through with loudly ringing blow."]
And below again

Cum galea longe jacuit caput[4].

["With one swift blow lopped off the head."]

No arms, limbs, etc. chopped off and lying by as
by this Monsieur Fréart prescribed in this his censure[5].

Such are the pictures which the (reciting epic) poet
draws.   But of which the first sort, marked (1), are
un-executable; the second indecent and against the
decorum in painting, and unimitable on the stage.
And for the former sort see again what a design Virgil
makes for a shield in the same place (lib. VIII.).   But
which neither basso relievo, claro oscuro, nor colours
can execute.   "Fleets with their officers aboard them

[1] Horace, *De Arte Poetica*, l. 185.   [2] Virgil, *Aeneid*, Lib. IX. 754.
[3] *Ibid.* l. 750.   [4] *Ibid.* l. 771.
[5] Fréart's *An idea of the Perfection of Painting*, tr. Lond. 1668, p. 48.

appearing distinct; nations and the gods drawn to battle; generals and particulars; aggregate and separate; near and distant; little and great."

Inveigh here (but with modesty and socratic irony) against High Church and Popish toleration and inquisition of that horrid representation (viz. crucifixion) and other saints adored in those agonies and made altar-pieces, church-ornament and for rock closets. Not our part here to censure (like true protestant[1] and zealous) the idolatrous part. On the contrary should we speak our thought we might incur some displeasure perhaps for diminishing the force of that terrible word idolatry (which we might confine perhaps to the material virtue, the relic worship only, indulging all else for vulgar's sake who will always frame the idol and might better have one painted beautiful to hand). But as to humanity and manners, sure I am, that this is all ill, injurious, and imbruing young minds in merely cold blood, massacre, etc. And here take occasion to recommend the genius of our nation against keeping anything in pain and putting out of pain, though otherwise so greedy of fighting spectacles, but not cold-blood. Above all praise our laws for rack abolished: no wheel. "Spectacle corrupts more than the example mends or terrifies."

22. Common Citations and Remarks.

In praise and as mere just character of the Greeks: Note the two passages of Cicero and of Livy, the first such a partial zealot, the second such a high admirer and lover of his nation. The first *ad Fratrem*[2], when governing in Greece: cum vero ei generi hominum praesimus, non modo in quo ipsa sit, sed etiam a quo ad alios pervenisse putetur humanitas. ["But when we rule over a race of men in which civilization not only exists, but from which it is believed to have spread to others."]

---

[1] *Supra*, p. 119.   [2] Cicero, *ad Fratrem*, Lib. I. *Epis.* I. 9.

The other of Livy, viz. Lib. 39. viii. Nulla cum arte earum, quas multas ad animorum corporumque cultum nobis eruditissima omnium gens invexit. ["Not with one of the many trades which his nation, of all others the most skilful in embellishing the mind and body, has introduced amongst us."]

Against libidinous[1] representation in plastic art. This reflection (in a protopope of a master): "If I have a servant, a dependant, a poor relation, or any friendly person much beneath me and at my command, unashamed even though lewd and licentious in my life to use such a one and employ him in such a base service! And shall I use my *art*[2], my *science*, thus and prostitute my head and pencil? Shall I scruple out of my respect and regard to dignity of person to give a bawd's, a pimp's, a pandar's part to one for whom I have but the least common esteem? And shall I use that divinity, muse, and personage, which is beauty and decorum itself in such a vile manner and to such vilifying purposes?"

See also the good reasons of the pragmatical author Monsieur Fréart de Chambray[3] of the loss and distinction of good painters from bigots (as Rubens graces by Madam de Guise or Monpensier: Quere which?). Though Rubens' graces not so great a loss. Well that they were not a Raphael's: the only painter fit. For even Titian not fit. No heroic, antique, learning, poetry, enthusiasm. A Guido fitter: had he understood much beyond *le air de tête*.

Aemilium circa ludum faber imus et ungues
Infelix...quia ponere totum
Nesciet[4].

["You will come across in the Aemilian school a worker in bronze of the lowest rank...unhappy... because he has no idea of representing a whole."]

This applicable to the architect, as well as statuary,

---

[1] *Supra*, p. 114. [2] *Infra*, p. 175.
[3] pp. 15, 16. [4] Horace, *De Arte Poetica*, ll. 32, 34.

and painter. You may know him (viz. the pseudo-
architect) by his extolling an inlaid floor : mighty nice,
draught (with collections of such) of the rails of a new
modern altar, or the mosaic work and incrustation of...
He is a mighty admirer of Pietro da Cortona, Carlo
Maratti, above a Raphael, or a Carracci. He even
abhors, etc. Such a one having spent three or four
years at Rome, and got the mimical action and tones
of the Italian with the idiom and phrase, comes home,
and the first thing you hear of him¹....

Penatibus et magnis Dis².

["The gods of household and state."]
From hence take occasion to speak of the *lares*,
little statues, portable concealable movables. Every
one's first religion, his family's, his private and peculiar
one; then "the publics³," which a man and partaker
and intelligent in such affairs, the community, and
common religion, i.e. the religion in common *proavis*
and *focis*. A perfect toleration⁴ for private worship
and public. No priest called: but master of the family,
his own; as in the main and in the higher degree the
magistrate himself for the public, the mere priests being
but servants⁵, one to a temple, a sort of sexton, little
better; and the augurs but a sort of pedlars in the
trade, not arrived to be such merchants and traders at
large as afterwards for whole kingdoms, continents;
as now the Jesuits (after gleaning up the remains of
other orders in the catholic Europe, where the whole
tribe of orders, etc. have in some kingdoms and states
swallowed two-thirds, and have gone so far as not to

¹ Continue this picture remembering Mr Talm-n.
² Virgil, *Aeneid*, Lib. 3, l. 10.
³ Letter of Enthusiasm, p. 17.
⁴ Not so at present (Turk and Christian) in Europe or Asia....Hard to
find in any region a human society which has *human* laws (Inquiry, p. 97).
This self-citation tempered as many others by an as I said to that Lᵈ P
elsewhere particularly when it refers to 'Letter of Enthusiasm.' For as
to the Inquiry, indeed, and other Tracts it cannot be so well said your
Lord P....
⁵ Miscellany, p. 43.

leave slaves now remaining, or a gentry and laity enough
to cover and guard them, or keep up the countenance
of a temporal and civil government) are gone to Asia,
China, America, joining real trade and commerce with
their spiritual, and bidding for the magi-empire, by a
previous universal monarch, their assured slave.

23. MORAL AND THEOLOGICAL CITATIONS AND MAXIMS.

1. The two passages of the Ἀπομνημονεύματα[1] of
Xenophon, Dialogue of Socrates with the painter and
statuary. Also with the armourer, *ibid.*

2. "Inquiry," pp. 104, 105, on the τὸ καλόν. A
principal and fundamental citation for plastic beauty
and contemplation.

3. Maxim, viz. Ruinous in religious and moral
sense to wonder or admire wrong. Hence superstition.
So barbarity (that of tyrants) from delight in blood,
pain, torture. First a horrour: then by degrees a
delight. At last horrour removed, delight remains,
etc. ἐπιχαιρεκᾰκία[2].

4. Thus in painting, wonderment, astonishment
at bold and great things apt to beget the taste of
savage and monstrous in design and colouring. And
the same wonderment and rapture at the sight of
pretty and genteel things apt to beget the little taste
or relish of toys, baby relish, womanish as Camilla's in
Virgil's *Aeneid*, Lib. XI. 775:

Tum croceam chlamydemque sinusque crepantes
Carbaseos fulvo in nodum collegerat auro,
Pictus acu tunicas et barbara tegmina crurum.

["Red gold knotted up his yellow scarf with its
rustling lawny folds; his tunics and barbarian leggings
were wrought in needlework."]

[1] Xenophon's *Memorabilia*, Book III. ch. x.
[2] This maxim may be placed under the head of Taste, *supra*, p. 108.

which was what Virgil here called womanish in
Camilla's taste, and which he makes to be her loss
and ruin, and of the whole cause and army entrusted
with her. Noble and just heroic fable of the same
sense and moral as that of Esop's kind of the Bride
and Mouse. "Nothing even of natural beings worthy
of wonder or admiration but as, etc."

Est aliquid quo tendis et in quod dirigis arcum?
...atque ex tempore vivis[1]?

["Is there anything whither you tend? and to what
do you direct your bow?...and do you live from the
Time?"]

Extemporary life miserable. Better the settled
miser or covetous passion (when attended with thought
of name, family, etc.), than the full, easy, contented,
but uncertain floating. *Non prescripta ad munia
surgit* (as the accumulator). But "what shall I do
next?" *Oscitantia*: visiting fashionable gentlemen of
the town, set up with a pair of horses and a chariot.
"Whither shall we go?" "How pass our time, till
such or such an hour, the opera play, etc.?" In the
interim caught by a thousand passions, hooks, snares:
always sure to catch those who are not engaged. But
the accumulator (though the worst employed) more
secure. The collector of a cabinet and intent virtuoso,
still more secure as nearer order, virtue, beauty. If
taken with a belle; for once or so only; not ever, not
a rake.

The unity and equality of life, made by unity of
object. Therefore the artist (if in liberal art) one of
the happiest men, whilst truly φιλόπονος and true
to his art. Capable of doing the greatest good (as the
intention of this treatise is to show). And therefore
worthy even of a liberal and noble born youth: if an
extraordinary genius, with particular reasons against
the public and family engagements (i.e. economy the

---

[1] Persius, *Sat.* III. l. 60.

chief part or duty of such person). And so Fabius Pictor in Pliny, with many other Grecians, if examined[1].

What Virgil[2] said of stealing verses from Homer: Facilis esse Herculi clavum quam Homero versum surripere: so a figure from a great master's piece in great design, viz. history and composition, where the fifth part (the collocation, just position and optics are observed) by reason of want of application. For how apply to any thing besides? How adapt but as there adapted; if the design be just, real, one, a whole?

Also the reason given by the French author, viz. Monsieur Fréart de Chambray[3]: "Si bien qu'il est absolument impossible apres avoir dérobé quelque partie du travail dans une nouvelle composition, sous l'aide de la perspective!" Now if perspective be called to assistance and the figure new designed, it is in great measure original and a new figure, at least much more so than anything taken from a statue. Since the figure borrowed from painting must first be reduced, as it were, to statuary and life by the borrowing painter or copyist; and thence from that idea new wrought and so transferred into his new composition, which is almost equivalent to an original design or drawing.

1. The most lovely thing in the world is love of one's duty, part. So of one's art[4] (quatenus) painter merely; and more quatenus ingenious, virtuous painter in humanity, etc. i.e. in reality quatenus poet, historian, philosopher.

2. The word Σχέσεις [attitudes] by the deepest moralists borrowed from statuary, anatomy, designing, and applied as the most significant term of art in morals.

3. The *quid verum atque decens*[5] of Horace little

---

[1] "Ergo examine." Also see what modern in Vasari, etc.
[2] See in his life by Tib. Claud. Donat.
[3] Not quoting him as not worthy because of his detraction, insolence, conceit, etc. and what he so ignorantly says against Raphael's Massacre, p. 457 and over censoriously and bitterly against Michael Angelo, p. 14.
[4] *Supra*, pp. 171 and 174.
[5] Horace, *Epist.* Lib. I. I. II.

understood (like the blundering Bishop Fowler in his answer to the Letter of Enthusiasm, p. 4, *scil*. Great Discovery, etc.).

4. The vita colour (*quisquis erit vitae*[1]) of Horace; as also his *operumque colores*[2], to be alluded to, commented and morally explained (with sublime and pathetic as may be) in the chapter[3] of colouring; the melting, uniting, counterposition, marriage, symphonizing, spreading, diffusing, communicating, conspiring of tints.

5. Mem[d]. The *malus musicus delitascens in choro*. Where is this? In Arrian? or...? Subjoin this as a reinforcement to what is noted (Char-cks, vol. III, p. 263). And apply this or rather introduce it where mention is made of Jordano[4].

6. Also that passage (a principal citation) in Moralists, p. 211: "Knowing as you are...well knowing in all the degrees and orders of beauty...of the particular forms, etc."

Learning music practically (as to play on an instrument, or sing, or anything of this kind beyond mere rudiments and for better speculation, theory, and ear, is the same in a gentleman or liberal youth, as learning to paint. 'Tis mechanical. 'Tis either poor and base, if indifferent and slightly studied (and as the French say sillily cavalièrement), or, if thoroughly and to perfection, requires the whole man[5].

But remember what as to statuary is feigned by the poetical author of Telemachus and Philocles, when compelled for a livelihood. One of the finest parts in his book.

Among other citations remember Marcus on the *rictus* of wild beasts, etc. (and here innate ideas).

Also Socrates on painting in the Memorabilia, instructing about the passions. Mark that painting

---

[1] Horace, *Satires*, Lib. II. Sat. I. l. 60.   [2] *De Arte Poetica*, l. 86.
[3] *Supra*, p. 148.
[4] *Supra*, p. 132. N.B. This ought to have been placed in common citations as being not properly moral in the use and sense.
[5] See what is said on this subject above, p. 112 and p. 115.

though high at that time as to symmetry, form, etc., yet not as yet attained this part of the affections, the pathetic, moral, etc.

"To look around, inspect, survey, dive into beauty, be present with nature in her sweetest aspects. See her causes and dependancies, her drawing, design, her prosperity (πᾶν μοὶ συναρμόσῃ, etc.), her flourishing, a beauteous perspective, the woods, the rivers, animals, birds (the rising singing lark), and thus joyously with the rest celebrate nature's festival, her birthday, marriage, progeny, and give joy to the incessant creator."

Self-cite the passage in Soliloquy[1]: "The Thalia's, Polyhymnia's, etc., willingly join their parts and being alike interested in the cause of numbers are with regret in favour of disorder—made syrens-pandar." So the generous painter—beware of fact, because of Titian's, Carache's and others prostitution. But keep to what *should* be, and to the example of the best ancients, the majesty and gravity also of a Roscius, an Aesopus in acting. See Cicero, what he says of one of them keeping to the grave and slow pronunciation: though not so popular and effeminate. See above[2] what is said on obscenity in painters.

Self-cite also on good occasion the theological passages referring to art in Inquiry[3]: "the elegant passion, or love of beauty running too high, etc." Ecstasy and rapture in the common subjects of art, etc. enthusiasm.

The rules of perspective lie hid (under the *je ne sais quoi*) like the rules of morals, right and wrong, equity and inequity, etc.

The philosopher and virtuoso alone capable to prove, demonstrate. But the idiot, the vulgar man can feel, recognise. The eye has sense of its own, a practice method peculiar and distinct from common reason or argumentation. Thus the equilibrium found

[1] p. 317.   [2] p. 171.
[3] Latter end of first book, viz. p. 75.

so instantly in some creatures (as that of the wing in a swallow and the legs in a partridge and other poultry kinds), as well as all their other instincts, which our kind made by nature to rely on reason (virtuoso-like and according to that rule of *frustra fit per plura*) possesses in a less degree.   But the anti-virtuosi again says—Who is he?—Who but the same one and the same man from him who said he knew not what the καλόν [beautiful] was εἰ μὴ ἐπαινετόν? [unless it be praised?]   Hence Hobbes, Locke, etc. still the same man, same genus at the bottom.—"Beauty is nothing." —"Virtue is nothing."—So "perspective nothing.— Music nothing."—But these are the greatest realities of things, especially the beauty and order of affections.

These philosophers together with the anti-virtuosi may be called by one common name, viz. barbar....

DICTIONARY[1] OF ART TERMS

In case of the word *ordonance* (necessary to be used as before in Letter and Notion) remember to put sometimes the word *economy*.

In case of the word *group* or *groups* (in the same manner) the word *mass.* "The groups, masses."

And in case of *plastic*, the word *graphic* (as in Sensus Communis, p. 146), especially when with a glance to *gravery-geo-graph*, Ars graph.

Also these words (some made, others already of art)

Ryparography } Pliny.		Feigned, devotional }	
Ryparographers }		Ecstatic, seraphic, mystic } Life.	
Accompaniments.		Grotesque, barbarous }	
Colourists, viz. of the Venetian School for the best.		Savage, monstrous }	
Mannerists.		Fruitage.	
Epic[2]-painting and painter.		Drapery.	
Contraposition of tints.		Groups or masses.	
The plastic[3].		Ordonance.	
Picturesque[4], grotesque.		Foreshortening.	
Arabesque.		High-low-side-short.	
Contrast.		Killing, killed.	
Tint for *teinte*.		Deadened, mortified.	
Machinery.		Tablature.	
Vegetable, still		Relief works.	
Sensible, quick }		Inwroughts.	
Real }		Outline.	
Natural, animal } Life.		Signature.	
Heroic, epic }		Designation.	
Tragic, poetic }		Figurative (as in the title).	
Masculine }		Freedom and free manner.	
Romantic, fantastic }		Style.	
		Design.	

(1) What to join with the word epique (for tragic) instead of comic and satire? The word not yet found. But remember the word *ethic* in case of moral and manners. Thus "ethic and moral," "ethic and heroic," "epic and ethic," "ethic artist, painter," "ethic and poetic."

---

[1] *Supra*, p. 7.

[2] P. Belloris' Raphael, p. 38.

[3] The generous plastic, the noble plastic (the artist). The epic master, heroic painter, etc. The maker, ποιητής, creator, etc. as in Miscellanys.

[4] But whereas the terminations in *esque* (as burlesque, romanesque, etc.) are all buffooning, remember never to use the word *pictoresque* by way of honour (as all common painters in their art, so Raphaelesque or Salvatoresque). But rarely this, and use instead of it painterlike, plastical, graphical, poetical.

The epic-painter can be said with dignity. But what for a Paul Veronese, an ordinary scripture painter, painter of Christ's, Apostles, virgins, etc.? Martyrdoms indeed are tragic in form and epic because usually intermixt with heathen grandeur, pomps, and magistrate, with the sublime of Christian machine and seraphim in the air, etc.

(2) Venture the word and call the *tablature* sometimes the *poem* after P. Belloris' example (p. 36, l. 8) of his pictures of Raphael in the Vatican.

(3) The epithetic decorous (under the head Decorum) and the *decorouse* instead of the *pulchrum*. τὸ καλόν as in sounds, the sonorous.

(4) The *virtual* for the virtuous; which last cannot be used for the energetic in the good sense. But virtual may be introduced with practical. Also applied to make things—painting, etc. For so already in our language the *virtue* of a medium, etc. Hence the *virtualize* to come in case (and with diversion) of virtuoso.

(5) In the same manner the numerous (sense of number). The decorous, the numerous (use them together). The true. The *verum atque decens* of Horace, *supra* p. 175.

INDEX OF EASE